YOUR
RETIREMENT

This book must be returned on or before

THE ROYAL BRITISH
LEGION

BECAUSE 200,000 CALLS FOR HELP EVERY YEAR CAN'T BE IGNORED.

Every year, the Royal British Legion goes into battle for the many thousands who, it seems, have served their country better than it has served them. We provide convalescent homes, counselling and rehabilitation facilities, resettlement and re-training courses, even pension advice. There is no charge for our services; the people we are able to help have given enough already. For more details, please phone 0171 973 7200.

REG. CHARITY No. 219279.

YOUR
RETIREMENT
HOW TO MAKE THE
MOST OF IT

THIRD EDITION

ROSEMARY BROWN

KOGAN
PAGE

First edition 1995
Second edition 1996
Third edition 1997

Copyright © by Enterprise Dynamics Ltd 1995, 1996, 1997

Kogan Page Ltd, 120 Pentonville Road, London N1 9JN

British Library Cataloguing in Publication Data
A CIP record for this book is available from the British Library.

ISBN 0-7494-2472-9

Typeset by BookEns Ltd, Royston, Herts.
Printed and bound in Great Britain by Clays Ltd, St Ives plc.

Contents

July 1997 Budget Highlights

Changes in expenditure taxes

- VAT on domestic fuel cut from 8 to 5 per cent, with effect from September 1997.
- Vehicle excise duty to increase by £5 to £150 from November 1997.
- Pack of 20 cigarettes to cost 19p extra from 1 December 1997.
- Alcohol duties to increase in line with inflation in January 1998: means extra 19p on a bottle of spirits, 4p on a bottle of wine and 1p on a pint of beer.
- Petrol raised by 4p a litre (18p a gallon) since Budget Day.

Homes and mortgages

- Mortgage interest relief to be reduced from 15 to 10 per cent from 6 April 1998.
- Stamp duty increased (July 1997) from 1 to 1.5 per cent on property sales above £250,000 and to 2 per cent on properties above £500,000.

Other key tax changes

- Tax relief on private medical insurance for people aged over 60 abolished: policies taken out, or arranged, before Budget Day – and actually paid for before 1 August 1997 – keep benefit of the relief until their renewal date.
- Dividend tax credit abolished: this will affect all pension funds immediately and, as from April 1999, PEP-holders and charities which, as a result of the change, will no longer be able to reclaim 20 per cent tax on their dividend income. While people with employers' final salary schemes should be protected, those with personal pensions in particular will need to invest more to make up the shortfall.

Small businesses and the self-employed

- Corporation tax cut from 33 to 31 per cent for larger businesses and from 23 to 21 per cent for small firms, with effect from April 1997.
- Capital allowances for small and medium-sized businesses doubled from 25 to 50 per cent for one year, from Budget Day to 1 July 1998.
- VAT threshold to be increased from £48,000 to £49,000 on 1 December 1997; the deregistration threshold will also rise from £46,000 to £47,000.

1

Planning Ahead for Retirement

Retirement today is a time of opportunity. Planning ahead helps to make the most of it.

Thanks to increasing life expectancy, a great many people can realistically look forward to enjoying 25 years, or longer, after leaving work. So, to be prudent, planning should include your eighties as well as your sixties.

This book is not designed to offer a blueprint. Its sole aim is to highlight some of the many choices, to advise on the best sources of information and to help you avoid the pitfalls that can trap the unwary.

Key concerns are likely to be the question of money and how you will occupy your time. Others may well include: where you live, how best to keep fit, the effect of your retirement on close relationships and perhaps new responsibilities such as the care of elderly parents.

You do not need to be an accountant to know that once you stop earning your income will drop. However, if you complete the Budget Planner (see page 21), you may well find that the difference is far less than you had feared. On the plus side, you will be saving on travel and other work-related expenses as well as enjoying a welcome reduction in tax.

You may also have savings: a lump sum from your pension and perhaps insurance policies. If so, it would be wise to draw up a plan for maximising their value. Should you invest your money in a building society, TESSA, unit trust or other outlet? Does it make sense to buy an annuity? What are the tax angles? If you are unsure of some of the answers, then the investment tips in Chapter 5 may help.

Your income may well depend on whether you get a new job. We are not pretending this is easy, but a great many men and women do in fact find rewarding work when they are well into their sixties.

A worthwhile alternative could be to devote your energies to voluntary work. There are scores of opportunities for retired people to make a valuable contribution within their own community. Whether you can only spare the occasional day or help on a regular basis, you will find lots of ideas in Chapter 9.

A prime requirement, whether you are thinking of paid or unpaid work, or for that matter simply planning to devote more time to your hobbies, is to remain fit and healthy. While anyone can be unfortunate enough to be struck down by an illness, the reason why the seventies are so often dogged by aches and pains is that sufficient care has not been taken in earlier years.

As well as all the obvious advice about not smoking or drinking to excess, there is the important question of exercise. While you could do press-ups and go for walks, you will probably have a much better time if you join the new keep-fit brigade. There are opportunities today for almost every kind of sport, with 50-plus beginners especially welcome. Additionally dancing, yoga and keep-fit classes are available through most local authorities.

The only problem is likely to be fitting everything in. The choice of leisure pursuits is little short of staggering. If you have ever wanted to learn about computers, take a degree, join a choir, become proficient in a craft or know more about wildlife, you will find an organisation that caters for your interest.

The type of activities you enjoy could be an important consideration in choosing where you will live. Because we tend to think of retirement as a time for moving home, many people up sticks without perhaps giving enough thought to such essentials as proximity to family and friends and whether a new area would provide the same scope for pursuing their interests.

While moving may be the right solution, especially if you want to realise some capital, there are plenty of ways of adapting a home to make it more convenient and labour-saving. You may also be able to cut the running costs, for example with insulation. These and other possibilities, including creating a granny flat, are explored in Chapter 7.

On the subject of granny flats, if you are caring for elderly parents there may come a time when a little outside help could make all the difference. The range of organisations that can provide you with back-up is far more extensive than is generally realised. While there may be pressure if a parent, however much loved, requires an undue amount of attention, a more common-place problem is the effect of retirement on a couple's relationship.

Many husbands are puzzled, and sometimes hurt, by their wife's attitude. For years she has been complaining 'I never see anything of you, darling' – so naturally he expects her to be delighted to have him at home. But according to some husbands, the enthusiasm may seem less than whole-hearted.

Put in blunt terms, many wives grumble that having a husband at home means an extra meal to cook. And while this may not apply in marriages where couples share the domestic jobs equally, in a majority of households women still do the lion's share of the cooking and cleaning. So, if he stays in bed longer, the chores will be finished later which can be an irritation. An even greater cause for resentment is that she may feel guilty about enjoying her usual activities unless her partner is also busy.

If she is still at work, the situation can be even more fraught as she may find her loyalties uncomfortably divided. Furthermore, quite irrationally, some retired husbands begin to imagine office romances that had never crossed their mind before.

Sometimes too, retired people subconsciously label themselves as 'old' and start denying themselves and their partner the pleasures of a happy sex life. It is difficult to know whether this is more ludicrous or tragic. As research shows, the sexual satisfaction of both partners continues in very many cases long after the age of seventy and often well into the eighties. A helpful book is *Living, Loving and Ageing*, price £5.99, from Age Concern and most bookshops.

Usually, problems that coincide with retirement can be fairly simply overcome by willingness to discuss them and to work out a solution that suits both partners.

Many non-marrieds also face tricky adjustments. Relatives may impose new pressures once you leave work. Close friendships sometimes alter when one friend retires – and not the other. Also, many people admit that they had not realised before how much they relied on their job for companionship.

Pre-retirement courses

Talking to other people can be immensely helpful. If you have not been lucky enough to attend a pre-retirement course but would be interested, the following organisations should be able to advise you.

The Pre-Retirement Association of Great Britain & Northern Ireland, 26 Frederick Sanger Road, Surrey Research Park, Guildford GU2 5YD. T:01483 301170. There are courses in both retirement planning and coping with redundancy. They are free from commercial bias and partners are encouraged to attend. Many local organisations affiliated to the PRA also run courses, details from the above address.

The Retirement Trust, 19 Borough High Street, London SE1 9SE. T:0171 378 9708. Free one-to-two hour seminars in all parts of the country.

Scottish Pre-Retirement Council, Alexandra House, 204 Bath Street, Glasgow G2 4HL. T:0141 332 9427. Runs courses in various parts of Scotland; prices from about £35 to £80.

Adult education centres. For information about local courses, see telephone directory under your local council listing.

Workers' Educational Association, Temple House, 17 Victoria Park Square, Bethnal Green, London E2 9PB. T:0181 983 1515. Many WEA branches run local courses. Contact branch office or the London HQ for information.

New focus for the retired

A number of organisations have been formed to represent the interests of retired people and to give them a more powerful voice in putting forward their views on issues that affect their lives. Three of the best known are:

Age Resource, 1268 London Road, London SW16 4ER. T:0181 679 2201. Promotes the concept that over-50s are not just capable of leading fulfilling lives but are an undervalued resource with a positive contribution to make. Among other activities, it runs an award scheme for projects and operates a network of Age Resource Desks to provide information about local opportunities for leisure, voluntary work and other outlets where older people can use their talents.

ARP/O50, Greencoat House, Francis Street, London SW1P 1DZ. T:0171 828 0500. Among other facilities, there are three free emergency helplines (legal, tax and domestic), a magazine and various social events. Membership costs £18 a year (£25 per couple) by direct debit.

National Pensioners Convention, 4 Stevens Street, Lowestoft, Suffolk NR32 2JE. T:01502 565807. The NPC is an umbrella group for pensioner associations throughout the country. Local subscriptions range from about 20p to £5 a year. For further information and addresses of local groups, write to the General Secretary at the address above.

2

Money Matters

For most people approaching retirement, the major concern is money. The fact that most of their friends who have already retired seem to manage pretty well is of little comfort. Even quite wealthy individuals confess to conjuring up images of going cold and hungry.

Happily, the reality is far rosier than many people imagine. The dread of drastic economies that haunts so many men and women is often due to their having only the haziest idea as to their likely income and expenditure.

Doing the sums

Knowing the facts is the first priority. To make a proper assessment, you need to draw up several lists:

- Expected sources of income on retirement
- Unavoidable outgoings
- Normal additional spending (including holidays).

Stage two, you need to consider options under the following headings:

- Possible ways of boosting your retirement income
- Spending now for saving later
- Cherished plans, if affordable.

Most difficult of all, you will require a third list of variables and unknowns which, while impossible to estimate accurately, must be taken into account in any long-term budget planning. The two most important are tax and inflation. Also, there are all the possible emergency situations such as your health for which, if this ever were to become a problem, you might want to make special provision. Your life expectancy is another consideration, as is that of your partner.

Ideally, you should start thinking about at least some of these points, especially those that relate to your pension, five or even ten years before you retire. When doing the sums, aim to be realistic. Many people make the mistake of basing their calculations on their current expenditure, without realising that some of their needs will change. It is a good idea to imagine yourself already retired. The good news is that, while some items will probably eat more of your budget, others will certainly be cheaper or no longer cost you anything at all.

Possible savings and extra outgoings are discussed below. The most practical way of examining the list is to tick off the items that you expect definitely to apply and, where possible, to write down the expenditure involved. See Budget Planner, pages 21–5.

Possible savings

When you leave your job, you will probably save at least several pounds a week. Items for which you will no longer have to pay include: your travel costs to work, bought lunches, special clothes; plus all the incidentals such as drinks with colleagues and collections for the Christmas party.

You will not have to pay any more NI contributions and, unless you choose to invest in a private plan, your pension payments will also cease. Additionally, when you retire, you may be in a lower tax bracket.

At the same time you may have reached the stage when your children are now independent, your mortgage is substantially paid off and you have stopped subscribing to a life assurance policy. Moreover, one of the advantages of reaching state pension age (or sometimes 60 for both sexes) is that you become eligible for a variety of benefits, e.g.: concessionary travel, free NHS prescriptions, cheaper theatre tickets (usually matinees) and a wide choice of special holiday offers. Also, many insurance companies give discounts to mature drivers. The normal qualifying age is 50 to 55.

Extra outgoings

There is no escaping the fact that when you retire some of your expenses will be heavier than at present.

Firstly, you will probably be spending more time at home, so items like heating and lighting are liable to be costlier.

If you received any perks with your job, such as a company car or health insurance, then these will have to come out of your own pocket in future. Any free business lunches will also cease.

Another important consideration is your extra leisure. With more time available, you will understandably be tempted to spend more on outings, hobbies and on longer holidays from home. To avoid having to stint yourself, these need to be budgeted for in advance. Even voluntary activity is not without its hidden expenses, for example: more use of the telephone, petrol costs, raffle tickets and so on.

Looking ahead, as you get older you may want more home comforts. Likewise, you may have to pay other people to do some of the jobs, such as the decorating, that you previously managed yourself.

Anticipating the areas of extra expenditure is not to be pessimistic. On the contrary, it is the surest way of avoiding future money worries.

Expected sources of income on retirement

Your list will include at least some of the following. Once you have added up the figures in the budget planner, you will have to deduct income tax to arrive at the net spending amount available to you.

- State basic pension
- State graduated pension
- SERPS
- Occupational pension
- Personal pension
- State benefits

You may receive money from some of the following:

- Company share option scheme
- Endowment policy
- Investments (stocks and shares, building society etc.)
- Bank deposit account
- National Savings interest
- Other existing income (from a trust, property, family business)
- Sale of business or personal assets

Unavoidable outgoings

One person's priority is another person's luxury – and vice versa. For this reason, the divide between 'unavoidable' and 'normal additional spending' (see section following) is fraught with obvious difficulty. For example, readers who do not possess a pet would never include pet food among the essentials, whereas a dog or cat owner unquestionably would.

Almost everyone will want to juggle some of the items between the two lists; or add extra outgoings omitted by us. What matters is the basic principle behind the exercise. If at some stage budgeting choices have to be made, decisions will be easier if you already know: your total outgoings, what you are spending on each and those you variously rate as important or marginal.

Whatever your own essentials, some of the following items will certainly feature on your list of unavoidable expenses:

- Food
- Rent or mortgage repayments
- Council tax
- Repair and maintenance costs
- Heating
- Lighting and other energy
- Telephone
- TV licence/rental
- Household insurance
- Clothes

- Domestic cleaning products
- Laundry, cleaners' bills, shoe repair
- Miscellaneous services, e.g plumber, window cleaner
- Car, including licence, petrol, AA, etc.
- Other transport
- Regular savings and life assurance
- HP/other loan repayments
- Outgoings on health

Normal additional expenditure

This may well include:

- Gifts
- Holidays
- Newspapers/books
- Drink
- Cigarettes/tobacco
- Hairdressing
- Toiletries/cosmetics
- Expenditure on pets

- Entertainment (hobbies, outings, videos, home entertaining etc.)
- Misc. subscriptions/ membership fees
- Charitable donations
- Other

Work out the figures against these lists. Then in order to compare your expenditure against likely income, jot them down on the Budget Planner.

Possible ways of boosting your retirement income

Other than luck, there are three main possibilities for providing you with extra money: your home, work and investment skill.

Your home

Your home offers several different options.

Moving somewhere smaller. You could sell your present home, move into smaller accommodation and end up with the double bonus of pocketing a lump sum and reducing your running costs.

The cash difference on the exchange will almost certainly be less than you hope. What with removal charges and lawyers' fees, moving home is a very expensive business. You may also have some decorating expenses and there is bound to be a short overlap when you will be paying two lots of telephone rental, extra electricity bills and so on. This is not to say that moving may not be an excellent decision; simply that, if money is the main criterion, you need to be thoroughly realistic when calculating the gains.

Ideally, you should try to dovetail selling and buying at the same time. If this is not possible (and it usually isn't), the golden advice must be to sell first rather than risk lumbering yourself with the expense of a bridging loan.

Taking in lodgers. If you have more space than you need, you could consider taking in lodgers, either as paying guests or, if your property lends itself to the creation of a separate flatlet, in a tenancy capacity.

You are allowed to receive up to £4,250 a year free of tax. **Tax relief only applies to accommodation that is 'part of your main home', so if you are thinking of creating a separate flatlet, you will need to take care that this qualifies and is not at risk of being assessed as a commercial let.** Check with your architect or other professional adviser that he/she fully understands the technical requirements.

Raising money on your home. You could part-sell your home either for a capital sum or regular payments, under a home income plan, and continue to live in it for as long as you wish. Sounds wonderful? There are both attractions and drawbacks. A solicitor's advice is essential.

Work

If you want to continue working, you might be able to stay in your present job and defer your pension. See 'Ways to increase your pension', page 29.

Alternatively, you may see retirement as the opportunity for a job switch or the chance to set up on your own. When assessing your budget plans, it is as well not to count on a splendid salary as – although this is improving – many 'retirement jobs' are notoriously badly paid.

If you are thinking of becoming self-employed or starting a business, you will not only have start-up costs but few new enterprises are immediately profitable.

On the other hand, while you are working you will not be spending money on entertainment. There may also be tax advantages and scope for improving your pension. Lastly, you may be one of the lucky ones for whom work after retirement really pays.

Investment

You do not need to be very rich, nor under 60, to start thinking about investing.

Investment can take many forms, with something to suit almost everyone. We do suggest that you at least look at Chapter 5, since maximising your income in retirement could make all the difference to your enjoyment of life.

Spending now for saving later

Although you may think that there is never a best time for spending, retirement planning is different in that sooner or later you will need, or want, to make certain purchases – or pay off outstanding commitments, such as a mortgage. Most people's priority list includes one or more of the following:

- Expenditure on their home
- The purchase of a car
- The termination of HP or other credit arrangement.

There may also be a number of purchases which you had been promising yourself for some time, with the only question being 'deciding when'. To help you assess whether a policy of 'spending now' is sensible, or possibly self-indulgent, there are two very simple questions you should ask:

■ Can I afford it more easily now – or in the future?
■ By paying now rather than waiting, shall I be saving money in the long run?

True, the issue may be more complicated, but for most choices this very basic analysis helps greatly to clarify the financial arguments on both sides.

Home improvements. If you plan to stay where you are, at some point you will probably want to make some changes or improvements: install central heating, insulate the loft, modernise the kitchen or perhaps create an extra bathroom.

Some people find it easier, and more reassuring, to pay major household bills while they are still earning. Others specifically plan to use part of the lump sum from their pension to create a dream home.

To find the answer that makes best financial sense, present commitments have to be weighed against likely future expenditure (together with what money you will have available). Equally, as with insulation, you will need to work out what long term savings you could enjoy by taking the plunge now. There is also the safety aspect: if you have bad lighting or dangerously worn carpet on part of the staircase, waiting a few years could prove very false economy.

Another important question is how certain you are that you intend to stay in your present home. Investing a fortune and then moving a couple of years later is generally a recipe for being out of pocket.

Purchasing a car. There could be two good reasons for buying a new car before you retire. One is that you have a company car that you are about to lose. The other is that your existing vehicle is beginning (or will probably soon start) to give you trouble. If either of these apply, it probably makes sense to buy a replacement while you are still feeling relatively flush.

Paying off HP and similar. In general, this is a good idea since delay is unlikely to save you any money – and may actually cost you more. The only precaution is to check the small print of your agreement, to ensure that there is no penalty for early repayment. A further exception could be your mortgage, as there may be tax advantages in keeping one. An accountant would advise you.

Extra income

There are a great many state benefits designed to give special help to people in need. This applies, among others, to problems connected with: health, housing, care of a disabled relative, widowhood and problems encountered by the frail elderly.

While many of these benefits are 'means-tested', i.e. are only given to people whose income is below a certain level, some, such as disability living allowance, do not depend on how poor or wealthy you are. Even when 'means-testing' is a factor, income levels are often nothing like as low as many people imagine. Because this is not widely enough known, many people are not claiming help to which they are entitled.

The main benefits and allowances are listed in their appropriate chapters. For more detailed information, see DSS booklet FB 2, *Which Benefit?*, available from any Social Security office; or ring your local DSS Freephone number (see telephone directory under Social Security or Benefits Agency).

Budget planner

Whether you are about to retire tomorrow or not for several years, completing the following Budget Planner (even if there are a great many gaps) is well worth the effort.

An imaginative tip, given to us by one of the retirement magazines, is to start living on your retirement income some six months before you retire. Not only will you see if your budget estimates are broadly correct but since most people err on the cautious side when they first retire, you will have the added bonus of all the extra money you will have saved.

1. Possible savings when you retire

Item	*Estimated monthly savings*
National insurance contributions	_____
Pension payments	_____
Travel expenses to work	_____
Bought lunches	_____
Incidentals at work, e.g. drinks with colleagues, collections for presents	_____

Item	Estimated monthly savings
Special work clothes	_____
Concessionary travel	_____
Free NHS prescriptions	_____
Mature Drivers' Insurance Policy	_____
Life assurance payments and/or possible endowment policy premiums	_____
Other	_____
TOTAL	_____

N.B. You should also take into account reduced running costs, if you move to a smaller home; any expenses for dependent children that may cease; plus other costs, e.g. mortgage payments, that may end around the time you retire. Also the fact that you may be in a lower tax bracket.

2. Possible extra outgoings when you retire

Item	Estimated monthly cost
Extra heating/lighting bills	_____
Extra spending on hobbies and other entertainment	_____
Replacement of company car	_____
Private health care insurance	_____
Life/permanent health insurance	_____
Cost of substituting other perks, e.g. expense account lunches	_____
Out-of-pocket expenses for voluntary work activity	_____
Other	_____
TOTAL	_____

N.B. Looking ahead, you will need to make provision for any extra home comforts you might want; and also, at some point, of having to pay other people to do some of the jobs that you normally manage yourself. If you intend to take out a covenant for a charity, this too should be included on the list. The same applies to any new private pension or savings plan that you might want to invest in to boost your long term retirement income.

Note on Table 3
Many people have difficulty understanding the tax system and you should certainly take professional advice if you are in any doubt at all.

However, if you fill in the following table carefully, it should give you a pretty good idea of your income after retirement and enable you to make at least provisional plans.

Remember too that you may have one or two capital sums to invest, such as:

- the commuted lump sum from your pension
- money from an endowment policy
- gains from the sale of company shares (SAYE or other share option scheme)
- profits from the sale of your home or other asset
- windfall profits from a building society.

3. Expected sources of income on retirement

A. *Income Received Before Tax*

    State basic pension   _____

    Graduated pension   _____

    SERPS   _____

    Occupational pension(s)   _____

    Self-employed or personal pension   _____

    State benefits   _____

    Casual or other pre-tax earnings   _____

    Total   _____

    Less Personal Tax Allowance and possibly
       also Married Couple's Allowance   _____

    The 20 per cent rate tax on the first
      £4,100 of taxable income   _____

    Basic Rate Tax   _____

    TOTAL A   _____

B. *Income Received After Tax*

    Dividends (gilts, unit trusts, shares, etc.)   _____

    Bank deposit account   _____

    Building society interest   _____

Annuity income _____

Other (incl. earnings subject to PAYE) _____

TOTAL B _____

TOTAL A + TOTAL B _____

Less Higher rate tax (if any) _____

Plus Other tax-free receipts _____

Investment Bond withdrawals _____

National Savings interest _____

Other _____

TOTAL NET INCOME _____

4. Unavoidable outgoings

Item	Estimated monthly cost
Food	_____
Rent or mortgage repayments	_____
Council tax	_____
Repair and maintenance costs	_____
Heating	_____
Lighting and other energy	_____
Telephone	_____
TV licence/rental	_____
Household insurance	_____
Clothes	_____
Laundry, cleaner's bills, shoe repair	_____
Domestic cleaning products	_____
Misc. services, e.g. plumber, window cleaner	_____
Car (incl. licence, petrol etc.)	_____
Other transport	_____
Regular savings/life assurance	_____
HP/other loan repayments	_____
Outgoings on health	_____
Other	_____
TOTAL	_____

N.B. Before adding up the total, you should look at the 'Normal Additional Expenditure' list, as you may well want to juggle some of the items between the two.

5. Normal additional expenditure

Item	Estimated monthly cost
Gifts	_____
Holidays	_____
Newspapers/books/videos	_____
Drink	_____
Cigarettes/tobacco	_____
Hairdressing	_____
Toiletries/cosmetics	_____
Entertainment (hobbies, outings, home entertaining etc.)	_____
Misc. subscriptions/membership fees	_____
Charitable donations	_____
Covenants	_____
Expenditure on pets	_____
Other	_____
TOTAL	_____

N.B. For some items, such as holidays and gifts, you may tend to think in annual expenditure terms. However, for the purpose of comparing monthly income versus outgoings, it is probably easier if you itemise all the expenditure in the same fashion. Moreover, if you need to save for a special event such as your holiday, it helps if you get into the habit of putting so much aside every month (or even weekly).

3

Understanding Your Pension

Next to your home, your pension is almost certainly your most valuable asset. It is therefore important to check all the angles well ahead of time to ensure that when you retire you receive the maximum benefit.

State pensions

You can get a pension if you are a man of 65 or a woman of 60, provided you have paid (or been credited with) sufficient national insurance contributions.

If you are an employee, your employer will have automatically deducted Class 1 contributions from your salary, provided your earnings were above a certain limit (currently £62 a week).

If you are self-employed you will have been paying a flat-rate Class 2 contribution every week and possibly the earnings-related Class 4 contributions as well.

You may also have paid Class 3 voluntary contributions at some point in your life in order to maintain your contributions record.

If you are over pension age (65 for men and 60 for women) you do not need to pay national insurance contributions.

If you have not paid sufficient NI contributions to qualify for a full rate basic pension you may be entitled to a reduced rate of pension. However, your NI contributions record will have been maintained in the following circumstances:

If you have lived outside Great Britain. If you have lived in Northern Ireland or the Isle of Man, any contributions paid there will count towards your pension.

If you have lived in a European Community country or any country whose social security system is linked to Britain's by a reciprocal agreement, contributions or residence there may count towards your pension. Your local Social Security office will be able to advise you.

If you have received Home Responsibilities Protection (HRP). This would be likely to apply if, since 1978, you had to give up work for some time to care for a child or for a sick, or elderly, person. See page 47.

If you have been in any of the following situations, you will have been credited with contributions (instead of having to pay them):

■ If you were sick or unemployed (provided you sent in sick notes to your Social Security office, signed on at the Unemployment Benefit office or had been in receipt of jobseeker's allowance);

■ If you were a man aged 60-64 and not working;

■ If you were entitled to maternity allowance, invalid care allowance or unemployability supplement;

■ If you were taking an approved course of training;

■ When you left education but had not yet started working.

Married women and widows who do not qualify for a basic pension in their own right may be entitled to some pension on their husband's contributions (see 'Pensions for Women' at the end of the chapter).

Reduced rate contributions note. Many women retiring today may have paid a reduced rate contribution at some time. Sadly this does not count towards your pension.

How your pension is worked out

Anyone wanting to work out what they are due can ask for a 'pension forecast'. For details on how to apply, see Form BR 19, obtainable from any Social Security office.

It is worth getting an early forecast as it may be possible to improve your NI contribution record by making additional Class 3 voluntary contributions. These can only be paid for six years in arrears, so this concession may not help if you think about it too late.

Your total pension can come from three main sources: the basic pension, the additional pension and the graduated pension.

Basic pension

The full basic pension for a man or woman (April 1997/98) is £62.45 a week, £99.80 for a married couple (unless your spouse is entitled to more than the £37.35 spouse's addition on his/her own contributions, in which case you will receive more).

All pensions are taxable other than one or two special categories, such as war widows. If, however, your basic pension is your only source of income, you will not have to worry about income tax.

The rate of basic pension depends on your record of NI contributions over your working life. To get the full rate you must have paid (or been credited with) NI contributions for roughly nine-tenths of your working life, although widows can also be entitled to a full basic pension on their husband's contributions. If you are divorced, you may be able to use your former spouse's contributions to improve your own pension entitlement, provided that you have not remarried before reaching pension age.

Your working life, for this purpose, is normally considered to be 44 years for a woman and 49 years for a man (i.e. age 16 until pension age), but it may be less if you were of working age but not in insurable employment when the National Insurance Scheme started in 1948.

Reduced rate pension

If you do not have full contributions but have maintained your contributions record for between a quarter and nine-tenths of your working life, you may get a pension at a reduced rate.

Additional pension

This is also known as SERPS, short for the State Earnings Related Pension Scheme. It is worked out on earnings since April 1978 on which you have paid Class 1 contributions as an employee. It is not applicable to the self-employed.

Class 1 contributions are paid as a percentage of earnings between a 'lower' and an 'upper' limit (currently £62 and £465 a week respectively).

How much additional pension you get depends on the amount of your earnings over and above the lower earnings limit for each complete tax year since April 1978. The current (1997/98) maximum to which you could be entitled is £109.04 a week. Full details and examples of how the additional pension is worked out can be found in leaflet NP 46 *A Guide to Retirement Pensions.*

As you probably know, if you think you can do better by making independent provision, you are not obliged to remain in SERPS. For details, see 'Personal Pensions' further in the chapter.

If you are a member of a contracted-out occupational pension scheme, you are legally entitled either to a pension which must be broadly the same, or better, than you would have got under the State scheme; or to what are known as protected rights (i.e. your and your employer's compulsory contributions to your pension together with their accumulated investment growth).

Graduated pension

This pension existed between April 1961 and April 1975. The amount you receive depends on the graduated NI contributions you paid during that period. Anyone over 18 and earning more than £9 a week at that time will probably be entitled to a small graduated pension. This includes married women and widows with reduced contribution liability. A widow or widower whose spouse dies when they are both over pension age can inherit half of the graduated pension based on their late spouse's contributions.

Ways to increase your pension

Deferring your pension. Your pension may be increased if you delay claiming it and instead continue working after normal retirement age. For every year that you defer retirement, approximately another 7.5 per cent will be added to your pension. This extra pension is paid either when you claim your pension or when you reach 70 (65 for women), regardless of whether you have retired from work or not.

An exception to the age rule sometimes applies in the case of a married woman over 65 whose pension is based on her husband's contributions. Her pension can continue to increase until such time as her husband gets his pension or reaches the age of 70, whichever is sooner.

For further details obtain leaflet NI 92 *Giving Up Your Retirement Pension to Earn Extra.*

Warning. If you plan to defer your pension, you should also defer any graduated pension to which you may be entitled – or you risk losing the increases you would otherwise obtain.

Increases for dependants. Your basic pension may be increased if you are supporting a dependent spouse or children. Most typically, this applies in respect of a non-working wife (or one whose earnings are very low) who is under 60 when her husband retires. It also applies for a retired wife supporting a husband dependent by reason of invalidity. For further information, see leaflet NI 196 obtainable from any Social Security office.

Age addition. Your pension will be automatically increased once you reach 80. The current rate is 25p a week.

Income support

If you have an inadequate income, you may qualify for Income Support. There are special premiums (i.e. additions) for lone parents, disabled people, carers and pensioners.

A condition of entitlement is that you should not have capital, including savings, of more than £8,000. To qualify for maximum income support, the capital limit is £3,000. For every £250 of capital over £3,000, individuals are deemed to be getting £1 a week income – so the actual amount of benefit will be reduced accordingly.

A big advantage is that people entitled to income support receive full help with their rent and should also not have any council tax to pay. See 'Housing benefit' and 'Council tax benefit', in Chapter 7.

If your only source of income is your basic State pension, you are likely to be entitled to income support. For more information, together with a claim form, see leaflet IS 1 *Income Support*, obtainable from any Social Security office or post office.

Social fund. If you are faced with an exceptional expense you find difficult to pay, you may be able to obtain a Budgeting or Crisis Loan, or Funeral Payment, from the Social Fund. Ask at your Social Security office.

Working after you start getting your pension

This used to be a problem for many people as a result of the Earnings Rule. At the time, men between the ages of 65 and 69 and women between the ages of 60 and 64 who earned more than £75 a week had their basic State pension reduced. Happily, this does not apply any more and today there is no longer any limit to the amount pensioners can earn.

Early retirement and your pension

Because so many people retire early, there is a widespread belief that it is possible to get an early pension. While the information is correct as regards many employers' occupational pension schemes, it does not apply to the basic State pension.

If you retire before you are 60, you may need to pay voluntary Class 3 NI contributions in order to protect your contributions record. Men over 60, however, automatically get contribution credits from the tax year in which they reach 60.

How you get a pension

You should claim your pension shortly before you reach State pension age. The Department of Social Security should send you a claim form (BR 1) but if this does not arrive, then it is your responsibility to contact them. They will send the form to the last recorded address they hold for you, so if you have moved and not informed them make sure they have your new address. You should apply for the form about four months before you are due to retire. If you claim your pension late, you could lose some of the money.

How your pension can be paid

If you live in the UK, you can choose to have your pension paid either by credit transfer or in order book form.

Credit transfer. This method gives you the choice of having your pension paid direct into a bank or National Giro account; or, alternatively, into an investment account with either the National Savings Bank or with most building societies. Payment will be made in arrears every four weeks, or quarterly, whichever you prefer.

Order book. You receive a book of orders (or pension book) which you can cash at a post office of your choice. Each order is your pension entitlement for one week and is valid for 12 weeks after the date shown on the voucher.

Other situations. Pensions can be paid to an overseas address, if you are going abroad for six months or more. For further details see leaflets NI 38 *Social Security Abroad* and NI 106 *Pensioners or Widows Going Abroad*, obtainable from any Social Security office. If you are planning to retire abroad and have any queries about your pension, contact the DSS Overseas Benefits Directorate at Longbenton, Newcastle upon Tyne NE98 1YX.

If you are in hospital, your pension can still be paid to you. You will receive a reduced amount if you are in hospital for more than six weeks. Leaflet NI 9 *Going Into Hospital* (from any Social Security office) provides full information.

Christmas bonus. This is paid with your normal pension at the start of December. The bonus is £10 and is tax free.

Advice

If you have any queries or think you may not be obtaining your full pension entitlement, contact your local Social Security office as soon as possible. If you think a mistake has been made, you have the right to appeal and can insist on your claim being heard by an independent Social Security Tribunal. Before doing so, you would be strongly advised to consult a solicitor at the Citizens' Advice Bureau or the Welfare Advice Unit of your Social Security office.

If you are writing to your Social Security office with a query you should quote either your national insurance number (or your spouse's) or your pension number if you have already started receiving your pension.

For further information about pensions, see leaflet FB 6, *Retiring? Your Pension and other Benefits* and booklet NP 46 *A Guide to Retirement Pensions* obtainable from any Social Security office.

Private pensions

Private pension schemes fall into two broad categories: those arranged by employers, e.g. company pension schemes, and those you can arrange for yourself. In both cases, investing in a pension scheme is one of the most tax effective ways of saving for the future.

- You get income tax relief on contributions at your highest tax rate.
- The pension fund is totally exempt from income tax and capital gains tax.
- Part of the pension can be taken as a cash sum when you retire and that too is tax free.

Company pension schemes

The basic points, which apply to all company schemes, are as follows.

Pension fund. Pension contributions go into a pension fund, run by trustees, which is quite separate from your employer's company. It is the job of the trustees to manage the fund and to ensure that the benefit promises are kept.

Payments into the fund. Your scheme may or may not ask for a contribution from you. For this reason, schemes are known as 'contributory' or 'non-contributory'. If (as is normally the case) you are required to make a contribution, this will be deducted from your pay before you receive it.

Your employer will also make contributions. In some schemes the amount is calculated as a fixed percentage of your earnings. In others the scheme actuary would estimate the amount that your employer needs to pay to ensure your (and other members') benefits in the future.

Benefits from the scheme. All pension scheme members should be given a booklet describing how the scheme works, what benefits it provides and other information including the address of the Pensions Ombudsman. You can ask to see a copy of the trust deed as well as the latest annual report and audited accounts.

The key benefits applicable to most pension schemes include:

■ A pension due at whatever age is specified by the scheme, usually somewhere between 60 and 65 (although many companies offer early retirement provision)
■ Death benefit paid out if you die before retirement age
■ A widow/widower's pension paid for life no matter when you die.

Benefit limits. The Inland Revenue sets limits on pension benefits which members of company schemes can receive. The main ones are:

■ The maximum pension you are allowed is two-thirds of your final pay (excluding State pension)
■ If you die, the pension can be passed on to someone else but no one beneficiary can receive more than two-thirds
■ The tax free lump sum, if you choose to take it, cannot be more than one and a half times salary.

The above figures are limited by a 'cap', currently based on £84,000 earnings a year. People earning less are not affected.

Types of scheme

Most employers' schemes are of the final salary or money purchase type. Other types that exist are average earnings and flat rate schemes.

Final salary scheme. Your pension is calculated as a proportion of your final pay. The amount you receive depends on two factors: the number of years you have worked for the organisation plus the fraction of final pay on which the scheme is based, typically 1/60th or 1/80th. So if you have worked 30 years for a company that has 1/60th pension scheme, you will receive 30/60ths of your final pay – in other words, half.

Final pay schemes can be contracted into or out of SERPS. If a scheme is contracted out of SERPS, it must provide a pension that is broadly equal to, or better than, its SERPS equivalent.

Money purchase scheme. Unlike final salary schemes, the amount of pension you receive is not based on a fixed formula but (within Inland Revenue limits) is dependent on the investment performance of the fund into which your own and your employer's contributions have been paid.

Different schemes have different ways of determining how members' pension entitlements are calculated, so enquire what the rules are.

An important feature of money purchase schemes is that the bulk of the fund must be used to purchase an annuity that will provide you with a guaranteed income for life. (See 'Compulsory purchase annuities', page 35).

Contracted-out mixed benefit scheme (COMBS). This is a mixed scheme, which combines elements of salary-related and money purchase schemes.

Average earnings scheme. This is based on your average earnings over the total period of time that you participate in the scheme. Every year, an amount goes into the scheme on your behalf, based on your earnings. Each year, your 'profits' are worked out from a formal table and the total of all these annual sums constitutes your pension.

Flat rate pension scheme. The same flat rate applies to everyone, multiplied by the number of years in which they have been participants of the scheme. So, for example, if the flat rate is £200 a year of pension and you have been a member of the scheme for 20 years, your pension will be £4,000 a year.

Compulsory purchase annuities

Everyone with a contracted-out company money purchase scheme (COMPS), AVC arrangement, personal pension, retirement annuity or Section 226 policy (explained on page 41), must by law purchase an annuity.

An annuity is an insurance product which guarantees an income for life. You can use the whole of your accumulated pension fund; or you can first take all, or part, of your tax free lump sum. If you take your lump sum, this will reduce the amount of annual income you receive.

You should take great care in choosing where you buy your annuity as the rates offered by life companies vary widely. Once you have made a choice, it is extremely difficult to switch.

You can take advice from an independent financial adviser, a pensions consultant or a company that specialises in tracking annuity rates. These include: **The Annuity Bureau Ltd.**, Enterprise House, 59-65 Upper Ground, London SE1 9PQ. T:0171 620 4090; **Annuity Direct**, 27 Paul Street, London EC2A 4JU. T:0171 588 9393.

Annuity deferral option. While most people have to buy an annuity as soon as they retire, people with personal pensions and members of small self-administered schemes can delay doing so up to the age of 75. Those who choose to wait can both take their tax-free lump sum as soon as they like after retirement and can also withdraw a limited income during the deferral period (i.e. until they purchase an annuity). However, there can be risks in withdrawing money, so expert advice is essential.

Additional voluntary contributions (AVCs)

AVCs are a very attractive way of making extra savings for retirement. Firstly, they enjoy full tax relief. They also allow you to purchase 'added years', to make up any shortfall in your entitlement to benefit under a company scheme.

You can get the same advantages with 'free-standing AVCs'. These are not linked to a company scheme but can be purchased independently from: insurance companies, building societies, banks and others. You are allowed to contribute both to company AVCs and to a free-standing plan or plans.

The total of all your AVCs plus other contributions to the pension plan is not allowed to exceed 15 per cent of your earnings. If you are already subscribing to company AVCs, check on your present level of contributions before investing in a new plan. In the event of over-funding occurring, the surplus will be refunded to you in cash, minus the tax relief involved.

For most people, the only problem with AVCs is the vast choice. You would be well advised to do some basic research into the track record of any policies you might be considering and on no account sign any document without first being absolutely certain that you fully understand all the terms and conditions including the administrative charges. In general, these are likely to be higher with free-standing contracts than for a collective AVC scheme offered by an employer.

Early leavers

In recent years the government has introduced new rules which give early leavers better protection. Even so, if you are thinking of taking early retirement you should work out very carefully how this might affect your pension. Most employers apply actuarial reductions. In other words you will receive less pension than if you had stayed till normal retirement age.

An important reform concerns what are known as your **preserved rights** – in other words, your financial rights with regard to your pension. Previously you only qualified if you had been in an employer's scheme for at least five years. Today the qualifying period is two years.

There are three choices available to people with preserved rights who leave a company to switch jobs. They can leave their pension with the scheme; take it to a new employer's scheme; or take it to an insurance company.

Leaving the pension with the scheme. You will receive a pension at the scheme's normal retirement age. Your accrued pension rights will be increased by 5 per cent a year or the rate of inflation, whichever is lower. Another advantage is that you keep any existing benefits. Also, once you start receiving your pension, you would be entitled to any extra increases that may be given.

Taking your pension to a new scheme. You do not have to make an immediate decision. You can transfer your pension scheme any time, provided this is over a year before you retire.

Early leavers can move their pension – or more precisely, its transfer value – to a new employer's scheme willing to accept it. The transfer value is the cash value of your current pension rights. Calculating this can be problematic and early leavers are often at a disadvantage compared with those who remain in the scheme.

Joining a new employer's scheme does not necessarily oblige you to transfer your previous benefits. In some circumstances, there may be an argument for leaving your existing benefits with your former scheme and joining your new employer's scheme from scratch for the remaining years that you are working.

Taking your pension to an insurance company. If none of the previous options appeal, or your new company will not accept your old pension value into its own scheme, you can go independent and have the transfer value of your pension invested by a life company into a personal scheme. After deducting its charges, the life company would invest the balance of the money in the fund, or funds, of your choice.

Advice. Deciding what's best is often very complex. Unless the issues are very clear-cut, expert advice is usually essential.

Becoming self-employed

If, as opposed to switching jobs, you leave paid employment to start your own enterprise, you are allowed to transfer your accumulated pension rights into a new fund. For most people the choice will be either to invest their money with an insurance company or to take a personal pension.

A third possibility which might be more attractive if you are fairly close to normal retirement age is to leave your pension in your former employer's scheme. See earlier para, 'Leaving the pension with the scheme'.

Useful reading. Pension Transfers and *Pension Opt Outs*; two very useful factsheets published by the Securities and Investments Board. Obtainable free from CABs.

Questions on your pension scheme

Most people find it very difficult to understand how their pension scheme works. However, your pension may be worth a lot of money and it is important that you should know the key essentials, including any options that may still be available to you.

If you have a query or are concerned about your pension, you should approach whoever is responsible for the scheme in your organisation.

The sort of questions you might ask will vary according to circumstance, such as: before you join the scheme, if you are thinking of changing jobs, if you are hoping to retire early and so on. You will probably think of plenty of additional points of your own. The questions listed are simply an indication of some of the information you may require in order to plan sensibly ahead.

Before you join the scheme

- Ask whether the scheme is contracted in or out of SERPS and whether the intention is that it should remain so in the future.
- How do you qualify to become a member? For example, there may be different conditions for different grades of staff. There may be an age ceiling for new entrants. Or a minimum period of service before you can join.
- Many companies have set up contracted-out money purchase schemes – or COMPS, as they are known for short – which operate on a different principle from final salary schemes. Ask what type of scheme you would be joining and if it is a money purchase one, how in particular members' entitlements are calculated. (See 'Money purchase scheme' page 34).
- If it is a final salary scheme, is it based on 1/60th, 1/80th or other fraction?
- Another point, if it is a final salary scheme, is what guaranteed pension increases are given? Since April 1997, schemes must by law give annual increases of at least 5 per cent or the rate of inflation, whichever is lower – but some schemes are more generous.
- Are discretionary increases given in addition to the guaranteed amount?
- Is anything deducted from the scheme to allow for the State pension?
- At what age is the pension normally paid?
- Are there any extra benefits included in the scheme?

If you want to leave the organisation to change jobs

- How much will your deferred pension be worth?

■ Should you wish to move the transfer value to another scheme, how long would you have to wait from the date of your request? (This should normally be within 6 months).

If you leave for other reasons

■ What happens if you become ill – or die – before pension age?
■ What are the arrangements if you want to retire early?
■ What are the rules/options regarding pension age for women if this has recently been raised to bring it in line with male pension age?

What to do before retirement

You may need to chase up any earlier schemes of which you were a member, as you could be due some extra pension.

Your previous employer/s may be able to help. If you draw a blank, best advice is to contact the Occupational Pensions Regulatory Authority (OPRA) which manages a pensions registry and tracing service to assist people who need help in tracing their pension rights. To request a trace application form (PR4), write to: **Pension Schemes Registry**, PO Box 1NN, Newcastle upon Tyne NE99 1NN. This is a free service.

Other help and advice

Other sources of help to know about are: the trustees or managers of your pension scheme; OPAS; the Pensions Ombudsman.

Trustees or managers. These are the first people to contact if you do not understand your benefit entitlements or are unhappy about some other point. Ask the pensions manager for names and addresses.

OPAS. This is a voluntary organisation which can help with any type of pension scheme – except State schemes. The service is available to anyone: scheme members, existing pensioners, those with deferred pensions and dependants.

The usual way of contacting OPAS is via your CAB. Or write to: OPAS Ltd., 11 Belgrave Road, London SW1V 1RB. T:0171 233 8080.

Pensions Ombudsman You would normally only approach the Ombudsman if neither the pension scheme trustees/managers nor

OPAS are able to help. The Ombudsman can investigate: (1) complaints of injustice caused by maladministration (2) disputes of fact or law. He cannot, however, investigate a complaint that is already subject to court proceedings or one that is about a State social security benefit.

There is no charge for the Ombudsman's service. The address to write to is: **The Pensions Ombudsman**, 11 Belgrave Road, London SW1V 1RB. T:0171 834 9144.

If you have a complaint about a personal pension, contact: **The PIA Ombudsman Bureau**, Hertsmere House, Hertsmere Road, London E14 4AB. T:0171 216 0016. It is possible he may refer you to the Pensions Ombudsman above but if so, you will be informed very quickly.

N.B. Many of the reforms contained in the Pensions Act came into effect in April 1997. These include the setting up of a new Occupational Pensions Regulatory Authority (OPRA) with wide-ranging powers to help ensure better protection for pension scheme members.

Personal pension schemes

Everyone – whether self-employed or working for an employer – has the choice of continuing with their present pension arrangements or switching instead to a personal pension (PP).

Although, most people over 50 are likely to be better off continuing as they are, if you are moving to a new job, are ineligible to join your company scheme or are thinking of becoming self-employed, one of the options described below may offer you an attractive solution.

Choices for the self-employed

Personal pensions are largely modelled on the old-style self-employed pensions – known as Section 226 policies.

These have now been abolished. However, anyone with an existing Section 226 policy is not affected – unless they actually wish to switch to a PP. As general wisdom, the view in the pensions industry is that for most people there would be little point in changing – and for some, it could be positively detrimental. But as with most decisions there are arguments on either side, so you should at least know what the choices are.

Differences between Section 226 policies and personal pensions. There are four main differences between Section 226 policies and PPs. These concern: the age of retirement, the method of calculating the lump sum, allowable contributions into the plan and the possible size of your pension allowed for tax relief.

- *Age of retirement.* Under a Section 226 policy, retirement cannot be taken before the age of 60. With a PP, you can retire at any time between 50 and 75.
- *Method of calculating the lump sum.* Under Section 226 contracts, this is expressed as three times the residual annuity paid. The PP rules define the amount as 25 per cent of the total fund excluding your protected rights.
- *Allowable contributions.* A Section 226 policy limits you to a maximum of 27.5 per cent of your earnings. For PPs, people over 50 can contribute up to 30 per cent, rising (depending on their age) to a maximum of 40 per cent.
- *Size of pension.* For high earners, the £84,000 cap is probably the strongest argument for hanging on to an existing Section 226 policy, since such policies are not affected by the earnings limit.

For further information, see leaflet PP 3 *Personal Pensions for the Self-employed*, obtainable by phoning the Pensions Line on 0345 313233.

Personal pensions for employees

You can take a PP in place of SERPS; or alternatively, in place of your employer's scheme.

If you are a member of a good contracted-out final salary scheme – or have the opportunity of joining one – it is very unlikely that a PP would be in your best interest.

If your employer does not have a pension scheme, if you are ineligible to join or if you think you could do better for yourself than under your current scheme, then a PP could be worth considering.

A main advantage of a PP is that if you change jobs you can take it with you without penalty. There are attractive tax relief benefits. You have a choice as to how your pension payments are invested and if you have built up a big enough fund, you can retire at any age between 50 and 75. Also, if you change your mind after having taken a PP, you can switch back into SERPS; or, if the scheme rules allow it, you can transfer your payments into a company contracted-out scheme.

Alternatively, if you enter pensionable employment but do not wish to transfer your PP to your employer's scheme, you can either leave it 'frozen' or transfer it instead to an FSAVC scheme.

The big drawback of a PP, particularly for an older person, is that it may not offer you such attractive benefits as your present scheme. Most employers do not make extra contributions to a PP so, other than your rebate from SERPS (see Minimum DSS contributions, below), all the investment towards your pension will need to come out of your earnings. You may also lose out on valuable benefits that are often included in an employer's scheme, e.g.: a pension before normal age were you to become ill; protection for your dependants should you die; attractive early retirement terms if you were made redundant; any increases in pension payments that the scheme may give to help offset inflation.

Before taking a decision, a first essential is to understand how PPs work.

Starting date. You can start a personal pension at any time and then, in order to receive all the DSS minimum contributions, backdate it to the start of the tax year on April 6. The formalities involved are very easy.

Contributions into your pension plan. There are three possible ways (previously four, see 'special incentive payments') of building up savings in your pension plan.

- *Minimum DSS contributions.* These will be paid into your PP automatically. They are worked out according to the level of national insurance contributions that both you and your employer are required to pay by law. The rebates vary with age: older people receive more.
- *Extra contributions made by you.* You can make extra contributions into your pension plan. If you do so, you will not only build up more savings but will have more flexibility as to when you can retire. If only the minimum DSS contributions are paid, you will have to wait until the normal State retirement age. If you make extra contributions, you can retire when you like between 50 and 75.
- There are Inland Revenue rules as to the amount you can invest, which varies according to your age. There is also a 'cap' on earnings – currently (1997/98) £84,000 – allowable for tax relief.

- If you are aged 35 or under, you can pay up to 17.5 per cent of your earnings into a personal pension.
- For ages 36 to 45: the maximum is 20 per cent.
- For ages 46 to 50: 25 per cent.
- For ages 51 to 55: 30 per cent.
- For ages 56 to 60: 35 per cent.
- If you are over 60, you can invest up to 40 per cent of your earnings.

Ages are calculated at the beginning of the tax year.

Relating back. This is a way of varying the timing of your payments. It is also possible to carry forward unused relief. Your financial adviser will be able to explain.

■ *Voluntary contributions by your employer.* Your employer might want to help you improve your pension by making extra contributions into your pension plan. Very few employers actually do so!

■ *Special Incentive Payments.* An extra 2 per cent payment was given by the government as part of the launch of PPs. These payments have now ceased. Anyone who previously received them can look forward to enjoying the benefit when they retire.

Your pension receipts. As with all money purchase schemes, the amount of pension you eventually receive will depend on two main factors: the size of the fund you have been able to build up and the fund's investment performance. You have a great deal of choice in the matter but there are also certain rules designed to protect you.

A basic rule concerns what are known as your **protected rights**. These are the DSS minimum contributions (including the value of the extra 2 per cent introductory payment) and tax relief you may have received – together with their accumulated investment growth.

Your protected rights can only be invested in a single contract and must be used to purchase the annuity which will pay for your annual pension when you retire. They cannot be used as a contribution towards your lump sum.

Your lump sum derives from the extra contributions that you – and perhaps also your employer – have made. You can take up to 25 per cent of this part of the fund. The remainder will be added to your protected rights to purchase a better annuity.

Choosing a pension plan. PPs are offered by insurance companies, banks, building societies, unit trusts, friendly societies and independent financial advisers (IFAs). Before deciding, you should aim to look at a variety of plans (see 'Types of Investment Policy', below). Also ask any questions about points that are unclear or technical terms that you do not fully understand – including in particular any questions you may have about the charges.

The law now requires anyone selling PPs to state their charges (including commission) in writing. Advisers must also put in writing their reasons for their recommendations to you.

Even after you have signed, you have a 14-day cooling off period to allow you to change your mind.

Useful reading. Leaflets PP1 *Thinking about a Personal Pension?* and PP2 *Making the Most of Your Personal Pension*, obtainable from Social Security offices or CABs. Leaflet IR 78 *Personal Pensions* from any tax office. *About Pensions*, DSS booklet explaining the difference between State, occupational and personal pensions – ring the Pensions Line on 0345 313233.

Types of investment policy

There are four different types of investment policy: with-profits, unit-linked, deposit administration and non-profit policies.

With-profits policies. These are one of the safest types of pension investments. They guarantee you a known minimum cash fund and/or pension on your retirement and, while the guaranteed amount is not usually very high, bonuses are added at various intervals.

Unit-linked policies. These are less safe but offer the attraction of potentially higher investment returns.

Deposit administration policies. These lie somewhere between with-profits and unit-linked policies in terms of their risk/reward ratio. They operate rather like bank deposit accounts, where the interest rate is credited at various intervals.

Non-profit policies. Although they provide a guaranteed pension payment, the return on investment is usually very low. Normally only recommended for people starting a plan within five years of their retirement.

Choosing the right policy. Great care is needed when choosing the organisation to invest your pension savings. Once you have committed yourself, you will not usually be able to change without considerable financial penalty. Before deciding, you should compare several companies' investment track records. look for evidence of good, consistent results over a period of 10 to 20 years.

Another point to scrutinise are the charges including commission you will have to pay. Normally, the best arrangement to keep the cost down is to pay a series of single premiums at one go or as a 'single recurring premium' contract.

A lump sum?

Members of company pension schemes and people with individual pension policies can take a tax free lump sum when they retire. The maximum normally permitted is one-and-a-half times average final salary.

Taking a lump sum reduces your pension but if you invest the money wisely, you could end up with a higher income. Alternatively, as many people do, you could use the capital for a worthwhile project such as improving your home.

Deciding whether a lump sum makes economic sense depends mainly on: your age, tax status, life expectancy – and whether you can manage on a smaller annual pension. It is not 'an all or nothing' decision. You can choose between: not taking a lump sum, taking the maximum allowed or taking just a portion (whatever sum you decide). An accountant or other financial adviser would help you work out the sums.

Pension rights if you continue to work after retirement age

When you reach normal retirement age, you will usually stop making contributions into your company pension scheme, even if you continue working. You will then probably have three choices:

■ You can continue working, draw your company pension and put some of your earnings into a separate scheme. People over 60 can invest up to 40 per cent of their earnings tax free into a pension plan.

Provided you joined your current scheme before 13 March 1989 (or an existing scheme where you were employed before 1 June 1989) you also have the following choices:

■ You can leave your pension in the fund where it will continue to earn interest until you retire. In most private schemes, you can expect to receive an extra 9 per cent for every year that you delay retirement.

■ You can leave your pension in the fund, as described above, and also contribute to a personal pension provided your contributions do not exceed the Inland Revenue limit.

Pensions for women

Women who have worked all their adult lives and paid full Class 1 contributions should get a full basic pension in their own right at the age of 60. The current amount is £62.45 a week.

Women who have only worked for part of their adult lives may not have enough contributions to get a full basic pension on their own record. Instead, they may receive a reduced pension or one based on their husband's contributions; or one topping up the other. A wife entitled to a reduced pension on her own contributions can claim it at 60, regardless of whether or not her husband is receiving his pension.

Married women who have never worked are entitled to a pension on their husband's contributions. In money terms, the value is about 60 per cent of their husband's basic pension. There are several important conditions, however.

Firstly, women can only get a pension based on their husband's contributions if he is in receipt of a basic pension. He must have reached 65 and have retired. Also, the wife herself must be over 60.

If she is still under 60 when her husband claims his state pension and does not work or her earnings do not exceed £49.15, he should be able to obtain a supplement of around £37.35 to his pension, on the grounds of having a wife to support. If the couple are living apart, the earnings limit for the wife is £37.35. Your Social Security office will be able to advise.

In contrast, if a wife has had her sixtieth birthday but her husband has not yet reached 65 (or has decided to defer his retirement), she must wait until her husband retires to receive her share of the married couple's pension.

Reduced rate contribution

Many women retiring today have paid a reduced rate of NI contribution, also known as 'the small stamp'. This option was withdrawn in 1978 but women who had already chosen to pay the reduced rate were allowed to continue. If you have only ever paid reduced rate contributions, you are not entitled to a basic pension in your own right but must rely on your husband's contributions for the married couple's pension.

Home responsibilities protection (HRP)

Men and women who have been unable to work regularly because they have had to stay at home to care for children and/or a disabled or elderly person may be able to safeguard their pension by claiming Home Responsibilities Protection. The person you are caring for must come into one of the following categories:

■ A child under 16 for whom you are getting child benefit
■ Someone whom you are looking after regularly for at least 35 hours a week, who is in receipt of attendance allowance, constant attendance allowance or disability living allowance
■ Someone – for example, an elderly person – for whom you have been caring at home and in consequence have been getting income support
■ A combination of the above situations.

HRP can only be given for complete tax years (6 April to 5 April), so if you simply gave up work for a few weeks in order to help out, you would be unlikely to qualify. Additionally, HRP cannot be used to reduce your total working life to below 20 years. To claim, ask your Social Security office for form CF 411.

Graduated pension. At best, this would only be a small amount. See page 29 for more detail.

Additional pension (SERPS). This too is described earlier in the chapter. See page 28.

Divorced wives

If you have a full basic pension in your own right, this will not be affected by divorce. However if despite having worked for a good number of years, you have insufficient contributions to qualify for a full pension, you should contact your Social Security office, quoting your pension and national insurance numbers. You may possibly be able to obtain the full single person's pension, based on your ex-husband's contributions.

Your right to use your ex-husband's contributions to improve or provide you with a pension depends on your age and/or whether you remarry before 60. As a general rule, you can use your ex-husband's contributions for the years you were married (i.e. until the date of the decree absolute). After that, unless you remarry, you are expected to pay your own contributions until you are 60.

If you are over 60 when you divorce, whether you remarry or not, you can rely on your ex-husband's contributions. If you remarry before 60, you cease absolutely being dependent on your former husband and, instead, your pension will be based on your new husband's contribution record.

A divorced man can rely on his former wife's contribution record during the years they were married to improve his basic pension.

For further information, ask your Social Security office for leaflet CA 10, *National Insurance for Divorced Women*.

Questions to do with occupational pensions on divorce are decided by the Courts. A judge could direct a pension scheme to make maintenance payments and/or to allocate part of a lump sum to an ex-spouse on the retirement or death of the scheme member. Provisions are in the pipeline to enable the Courts to require couples to share their occupational/personal pensions at the time of divorce; this is expected to become law by the year 2000.

Separated wives

Even if you have not lived together for several years, from a national insurance point of view you are still considered to be married. The normal pension rules apply including the fact that, if you have to depend on your husband's contributions, you will not be able to get a pension until he is both 65 and in receipt of his own pension.

If you are not entitled to a State pension in your own right, you will receive the dependant's rate of benefit. Once you are 60, you can draw the wife's pension of £37.35 a week, without reference to your husband.

If you are under 60 but your husband has reached 65 and is retired, he may be able to claim a dependency addition of £37.35 for you. He will not be able to do so if you are earning more than £37.35 a week.

If your husband dies, you will be entitled to widow's benefit in the same way as any other widow.

Widows

There are three important benefits to which widows may be entitled: widows' payment, widows' pension and widowed mother's allowance. To claim these, fill in Form BW1, obtainable from any Social Security office.

Widows' pension. There are various levels of widows' pension: full rate and age-related.

Full-rate widows' pension is paid to widows between the ages of 55 and 59 inclusive. The weekly amount is £62.45, which is the same pension as that received by a single person.

Age-related widows' pension is payable to a widow aged between 45 and 54 inclusive when her husband dies; or when she ceases to receive widowed mother's allowance. Rates depend on age and vary from £18.74 for 45 year olds to £58.08 for those aged 54.

Widows' pension is normally paid automatically once you have sent off your completed form BW 1. In the event of your being ineligible, due to insufficient NI contributions having been paid, you may be entitled to receive some other benefit. Your Social Security office will advise you.

Widows who remarry, or live with a man as his wife, cease to receive widows' pension unless they are aged 60 or over.

For further information, see leaflet NP 45 *A Guide to Widows' Benefits*. See also Chapter 12, pages 184–5.

4

You May Pay Less Tax in Retirement

Unfortunately, much as we should like to leave this out, the taxman never seems to retire!

Unless you are on a very low income, you will almost certainly be paying income tax and possibly one or two other varieties of tax as well. Although for most retired people the issues are not particularly complex, a little basic knowledge can be invaluable.

Firstly, it will help you to calculate how much money (after deduction of tax) you will have available to spend. Understanding the broad principles could also help you save money, by not paying more in taxation than you need.

If you are lucky enough to be fairly wealthy or if some of the recent Budget changes give you cause to wonder whether you are managing your money as tax-efficiently as you might, you should talk to an accountant.

Income tax

This is calculated on all (or nearly all) your income, after deduction of your personal allowance; and in the case of married people, of the married couple's allowance. The reason for saying 'nearly all' is that some income you may receive is tax free: types of income on which you do not have to pay tax are listed a little further on.

Most income, however, counts and you will be assessed for income tax on: your pension, interest you receive from most types of savings, dividends from investments, any earnings (even if these are only from casual work) plus rent from any lodgers, if the amount you receive exceeds £4,250 a year. Many social security benefits are also taxable.

The tax year runs from 6 April to 5 April the following year, so the amount of tax you pay in any one year is calculated on the income you receive (or are deemed to have received) between these two dates.

There are three different rates of income tax: the 20 per cent rate which applies to the first £4,100 of your taxable income; the 23 per cent basic rate tax which applies to the next slice of taxable income between £4,100 and £26,100; and the 40 per cent higher rate tax which is levied on all taxable income over £26,100.

All income tax payers will pay the 20 per cent rate on their first £4,100 of taxable income. Or put another way, for every £100 of your income that counts for income tax purposes up to £4,100, you have to pay £20 to the Exchequer – and are allowed to keep the remaining £80. If you are a basic rate taxpayer, the amount you have to pay the Exchequer increases (after the first £4,100) to £23; and if you are a higher rate taxpayer, it goes up to £40 for every £100 of your taxable income over £26,100.

In most Budgets, some of the figures change. Those quoted above – and elsewhere in the chapter – apply to the 1997/98 tax year.

Tax allowances

Personal allowance

Income tax is not levied on every last penny of your money. There is a certain amount you are allowed to keep before income tax becomes applicable. This is known as your personal allowance. Therefore, when calculating how much tax you will have to pay in any one year, you should first deduct from your total income the amount represented by your personal allowance (plus any additional or other tax allowance to which you may be entitled, see sections following). If your income is no higher than your personal allowance (or total of these allowances), you will not have to pay any income tax.

Everyone receives the same basic personal allowance, regardless of whether they are male, female, married or single; and regardless of whether any income they have comes from earnings, an investment, their pension or other source.

■ The basic personal allowance (1997/98) is £4,045.

People aged 65 and over may be entitled to a higher personal allowance, by virtue of their age. Those aged 75 and above may receive even more generous treatment.

The full amount is only given to people whose income does not exceed £15,600. People with higher incomes will have their age allowance reduced by £1 for every £2 of income above the income limit. But however large your income, your personal allowance can never be reduced below the basic personal allowance.

For those aged 65 to 74:
■ personal allowance is increased to £5,220.

For those aged 75 and older:
■ personal allowance is increased to £5,400.

N.B. Extra allowance linked to age is normally given automatically. If you are not receiving it but believe you should be doing so, you should write to your local tax office (see under Inland Revenue in the telephone directory) stating your age and, if married, that of your partner. If you have been missing out, you may be able to claim back anything you have lost for up to six years and should receive a tax rebate. The amounts have been altered several times since 1991/92, so any rebate would only apply to allowances that would have been due to you at the time.

Married couple's allowance

This is an extra allowance which, provided they live together, is given to all married couples.

At one time, the allowance normally went automatically to the husband. Today, however, couples can decide for themselves how they want the allowance to be used. They can leave it with the husband; choose to divide it equally; or allocate the whole allowance to the wife. The wife, if she so wishes, can claim half the allowance as of right. Couples who want all or half of the allowance to go to the wife will need to arrange the transfer through their tax offices, by completing Form 18. This will need to be done before the start of the tax year, i.e. before April 6. For address of your tax office, see Inland Revenue in the telephone directory.

As with the personal allowance, older people enjoy a more generous married couple's allowance. Increases are given when the husband or wife reaches 65, with a bigger increase still at 75.

Similar to (age-related) personal allowance, the married couple's age related increases are subject to a couple's income – so it is possible that they might not get anything extra at all.

A further point to note is that the option of transferring half, or all, the allowance to the wife only applies to the basic married couple's allowance – and not to the age-related addition.

The current (1997/98) married couple's allowance, together with the ceiling limits for the higher allowance, is as follows:

■ The basic married couple's allowance is £1,830.
■ When the husband or wife reaches 65, the allowance is increased to £3,185. The ceiling is £20,660.
■ When the husband or wife reaches 75, the allowance is increased to £3,225. The ceiling is £21,100.

N.B. Two important points you should know:

■ Married couple's allowance is restricted to 15 per cent tax relief.
■ Additions for age are normally given automatically. If couples are not receiving any extra but believe they should be, the husband should write to their local tax office stating their ages. If there has been a mistake, he will be given a rebate.

Widow's bereavement allowance. This is an extra allowance, worth £1,830 a year at current rates, specially given to widows to assist them over the first difficult period. The only qualification is that a widow's late husband must have been entitled to the married couple's allowance at the time of his death. The allowance is given both in the tax year she became widowed and in the following tax year.

As with other tax allowances, this is not a cash benefit that can be claimed at the post office. It is an offset against income, before calculation of tax. A widow would therefore be entitled to the total of her personal allowance and widow's bereavement allowance before her income would start to be assessed for tax. She would also be entitled to any unused portion of the married couple's allowance in the year her husband dies. If a widow is aged 65 or over, she may also be able to claim the age-related addition (see 'personal allowance' above).

N.B. Widow's bereavement allowance is restricted to 15 per cent tax relief.

Other tax allowances. Extra tax reliefs can also be claimed in a couple of other circumstances.

Additional personal allowance (single parent's allowance). This can be claimed by any parent bringing up dependent children on their own. The (1997/98) value of the allowance is £1,830 a year. N.B. A married man whose wife is totally incapacitated can also claim this allowance, in addition to the married couple's allowance, if he has dependent children living at home. The tax relief is restricted to 15 per cent.

Registered blind people can claim an allowance of £1,280 a year. If both husband and wife are registered as blind, they can each claim the allowance.

If you think you might be entitled to either of the above, you should write to your local tax office with full relevant details of your situation. As with age-related additions, if you were entitled to receive the allowance earlier but for some reason missed out, you may be able to obtain a tax rebate.

Useful reading

For more detailed information about tax allowances, see the following Inland Revenue leaflets obtainable free from any tax office (see under Inland Revenue in the telephone directory).

- IR 80 *Income Tax: A Guide for Married Couples*
- IR 90 *Tax Allowances and Reliefs*
- IR 91 *A Guide for Widows and Widowers*
- IR 121 *Income Tax and Pensioners*

Tax relief

Separate from any personal allowances, you can obtain tax relief on the following:

- Interest payments on the first £30,000 of a mortgage paid on your own home (see note below).
- A covenant for the benefit of a charity; or donation under the Gift Aid Scheme
- Contributions to occupational pensions, self-employed pension plans and other personal pensions
- Some maintenance payments, if you are divorced or separated.
- Private medical insurance for those aged 60 and over.

Mortgage interest relief. Tax relief on mortgage interest payments is restricted to 15 per cent. This applies to both existing and new loans used for home purchase.

Loans secured on an older person's (65 years or over) home which are used to purchase a life annuity receive tax relief at the basic rate.

Self-employed and other personal pension plans. There are different rules for personal pensions (PPs) and retirement annuity contracts. Retirement annuity contracts are personal pension schemes started before 1 July 1988.

With a PP, you can pay the following amounts into your pension scheme and obtain tax relief:

■ if you are aged 35 or under, 17.5 per cent of your earnings (up to a ceiling of £84,000)
■ between the ages of 36 and 45, 20 per cent of your earnings
■ between the ages of 46 and 50, 25 per cent
■ between the ages of 51 and 55, 30 per cent
■ between the ages of 56 and 60, 35 per cent
■ ages 61 and over, 40 per cent

With a retirement annuity contract, you can pay the following amounts and obtain tax relief (unlike PPs, there is no ceiling figure):

■ if you are aged 50 or under, 17.5 per cent of your earnings
■ between the ages of 51 and 55, 20 per cent
■ between the ages of 56 and 60, 22.5 per cent
■ ages 61 and over, 27.5 per cent.

Ages are calculated at the beginning of the tax year.

Maintenance payments. The rules were considerably simplified in the 1988 Budget, and, except for previous maintenance arrangements, are now as follows:

■ Individuals receiving payments are exempted from income tax
■ Individuals paying maintenance receive tax relief at 15 per cent on the first £1,830 of payments to a divorced or separated spouse; other maintenance payments, including any to children, do not qualify for tax relief.

Private medical insurance. People over 60 can get tax relief, at basic rate, on private medical insurance. Relief is available whether premiums are paid by the insured person or paid by someone else (for example a relative) on their behalf.

For further information, see leaflet IR 103 *Tax Relief for Private Medical Insurance* available from any tax office.

Tax-free income

Some income you may receive is entirely free of tax. It is not taxed at source. You do not have to deduct it from your income, as in the case of personal allowances. Nor do you have to go through the formality of claiming relief on it.

If you receive any of the following, you can forget about the tax angle altogether – at least as regards these particular items:

- Disability living allowance
- Industrial injuries disablement pension
- Income support (in some circumstances, e.g. when the recipient is also getting jobseeker's allowance, income support would be taxable)
- Housing benefit
- Council tax benefit
- Any extra which may be added to your state pension if you support children under 16
- All pensions paid to war widows (plus any additions for children)
- Pensions paid to victims of Nazism
- Certain disablement pensions from the armed forces, police, fire brigade and merchant navy
- Annuities paid to the holders of certain gallantry awards
- £10 Christmas bonus (paid to pensioners)
- National Savings Premium Bond prizes
- SAYE bonuses
- Winnings on the football pools and on other forms of betting
- Rental income of up to £4,250 a year from letting out rooms in your home.

Other tax-free money

The following are not income, in the sense that they are more likely to be 'one off' rather than regular payments. However, as with the above list they are tax free:

- Virtually all gifts (in certain circumstances you could have to pay tax if the gift is above £3,000 or if, as may occasionally be the case, the money from the donor has not been previously taxed).
- Redundancy payment, or a golden handshake in lieu of notice, up to the value of £30,000.

- Lump sum commuted from a pension with a maximum figure of £126,000.
- A matured endowment policy.
- Accumulated interest from a Tax Exempt Special Savings Account (TESSA) held for 5 years.
- Dividends on investments held in a Personal Equity Plan (PEP).
- Compensation money paid to people who were mis-sold personal pensions.

Income tax on savings

Since the start of the April 1996-97 tax year, basic rate taxpayers have enjoyed a reduction in tax on their bank and building society interest. Instead of paying the full basic rate, the amount charged is only 20 per cent.

Higher rate taxpayers continue, as before, to pay tax at 40 per cent.

People paying tax at the 20 per cent rate who previously needed to complete a form to obtain a repayment for the excess tax that had been deducted no longer have any need to worry.

Income tax on other investments

For most investments on which you are likely to receive dividends, tax will already have been deducted before the money is paid to you.

If you are a basic rate taxpayer, the money you receive will be yours in its entirety and you will not have to worry about making deductions for tax.

If you only pay tax at the 20 per cent rate, you will be able to claim a repayment from the Inland Revenue.

If you pay tax at the higher rate, you will have to pay some additional tax and should allow for this in your budgeting.

Exceptionally, there are one or two types of investment where the money is paid to you gross – without the basic rate tax deducted. These include National Savings income bonds, deposit bonds, capital bonds, the NS Investment Account and also certain specialist types of gilts. As with higher rate taxpayers, you will need to save sufficient money to pay the tax on the due date.

Abolition of composite rate tax. Since April 1991, non-taxpayers (people whose taxable income is less than their allowances) can request institutions such as banks and building societies to pay any interest owing to them gross, without deduction of tax at source. This is benefiting in particular many married women and pensioners who, although not liable for tax, were losing money through the composite rate tax system.

Many people who stand to benefit are still continuing to pay tax unnecessarily. If you have been missing out, simply request form R85 from the institution in question, which you will then need to complete. People with more than one bank or building society account will need a separate form for each account. Forms are also included in the Inland Revenue explanatory leaflet IR 110 *A Guide for People with Savings,* obtainable from any tax office or from your bank/building society.

People who have filled in an R85 should automatically receive their interest gross. If your form was not completed in time, you can reclaim the tax from your tax office after the end of the tax year in April. Leaflet IR 110 (see above) explains how to do this.

Reclaiming tax overpaid

If your income consists mainly of taxed investments, you can set your personal allowances against the income. You will quite likely be entitled to a tax rebate.

If you think you could be paying too much tax, you should obtain Tax Claim Form R40 from your local tax office (under Inland Revenue in the telephone directory). Complete the form and return it to the tax office, together with the tax vouchers concerned.

If you are claiming a repayment for the first time, fill in form R95 attached to leaflet IR 110 and send it to your local tax office. For further information see IR leaflet 110 above.

Mistakes by the Inland Revenue

The Inland Revenue sometimes also makes mistakes. Normally, if they have charged you insufficient tax and later discover the error, they will send you a supplementary demand requesting the balance owing. However, under a provision known as the 'Official Error Concession', if the mistake was due to a fault by the Inland Revenue, it is possible that you may be excused the arrears. However, you would need to convince the IR that you could reasonably have believed your tax affairs were in order. Also, the IR would need to have been tardy in notifying you of the arrears (i.e. more than 12 months after the end of the tax year in which the IR received the information indicating that more tax was due).

As part of the Citizen's Charter, the Inland Revenue has appointed an independent Adjudicator to examine taxpayers' complaints about their dealings with the Revenue.

Complaints appropriate to the Adjudicator are mainly limited to the way the Inland Revenue has handled someone's tax affairs, for example: excessive delay, errors, discourtesy or how discretion has been exercised. In deciding fair treatment, the Adjudicator has power to recommend the waiving of a payment or even the award of compensation if, as a result of error by the Inland Revenue, the complainant had incurred professional fees or other expenses.

Before approaching the Adjudicator, taxpayers will be expected to have tried resolving the matter with their local tax office or, if this fails, with the Regional Office.

For further information, see IR booklet, Code of Practice 1, *Mistakes by the Inland Revenue*, available from tax offices.

Or contact the Adjudicator's office for information about referring a complaint. The address is: **The Adjudicator's Office**, 3rd Floor, Haymarket House, 28 Haymarket, London SW1Y 4SP. T:0171 930 2292.

Tax rebates

When you retire, you may be due for a tax rebate. If you are, this would normally be paid automatically, especially if you are getting a pension from your last employer. The matter could conceivably be overlooked: either if (instead of from your last employer) you are due to get a pension from an earlier employer; or if you will only be receiving a State pension – and not a company pension in addition.

In either case, you should ask your employer for a P45 Form. Then, either send it – care of your earlier employer – to the pension fund trustees; or, if you are only getting a State pension, send it to the tax office together with details of your age and the date you retired. Ask your employer for the address of the tax office to which you should write.

Useful reading
For further information about income tax, see the following Inland

Revenue leaflets, available from any tax office:

- IR 92 *Income Tax: A Guide for One-Parent Families*
- IR 93 *Income Tax – Separation, Divorce and Maintenance Payments*
- IR 34 *Income Tax – Pay As You Earn*
- IR 56/NI 39 *Employed or Self-Employed*
- IR 65 *Giving to Charity – How Individuals Can Get Tax Relief*
- IR 123 *Mortgage Interest Relief: Buying Your Home.*

Post-war credits

Post-war credits are extra tax that people had to pay in addition to their income tax between April 1941 and April 1946. The extra tax was treated as a credit to be repaid after the war. People who paid credits were given certificates showing the amount actually paid.

In cases where the original credit holder has died without claiming repayment and the Post War Credit certificate is still available, repayment can be made to the next of kin or personal representative of the estate.

Interest is payable on all claims at a composite rate of 38 per cent. The interest is exempt from income tax.

All claims should be sent to the **Special Post War Credit Claim Centre** at: Inland Revenue, HM Inspector of Taxes – PWC Centre V, TY Glas, Llanishen, Cardiff CF4 5TX.

Capital gains tax (CGT)

You may have to pay capital gains tax if you make a profit (or to use the proper term, gain) on the sale of a capital asset, for example: stocks and shares, jewellery, any property that is not your main home and other items of value.

CGT only applies to the actual gain you make, so if you buy shares to the value of £25,000 and sell them later for £35,000 the taxman will only be interested in the £10,000 profit you have made.

Not all your gains are taxable. There is an exemption limit of £6,500 a year: so if during the year your total gains amount to £7,000, tax would only be levied on £500. Also, since 1982, the burden of CGT has been eased by the welcome introduction of indexation to offset the effect of inflation.

Additionally, certain items are free altogether of capital gains tax; and others, such as the sale of a family business, get special treatment. Details are given a little further on.

A very important point for married couples to know is that as a result of independent taxation each partner enjoys his/her own annual exemption of £6,500. This means in effect that, provided both partners are taking advantage of their full exemption limit, a couple can make gains of £13,000 a year free of capital gains tax. However, it is not possible to use the losses of one spouse to cover the gains of the other.

Transfers between husband and wife are tax free, although any income arising from such a gift will of course be taxed. Income would normally be treated as the recipient's for tax purposes unless, that is, the donor has the right to get the asset back in the future or retains some control over it – in which case the donor would be liable for any tax.

Gains are treated as a person's 'top slice' of income and are accordingly taxed at: 20 per cent (the lower rate), 23 per cent (basic rate), 40 per cent (higher rate) or a mixture of rates, i.e. in instances where a gain, or gains, pushes part of an individual's income into a higher rate bracket.

Free of capital gains tax

The following assets are not subject to capital gains tax and do not count towards the £6,500 gains you are allowed to make:

- Your main home (but, see note below)
- Your car
- Personal belongings up to the value of £6,000 each
- Proceeds of a life assurance policy (in most circumstances)
- Profits on British Government stocks
- National Savings Certificates
- SAYE contracts
- Building society savings
- Futures and options in gilts and qualifying corporate bonds
- Personal Equity Plan scheme
- Premium Bond winnings
- Football pool and other bettings winnings
- Gifts to registered charities
- Small part disposals of land (limited to 5 per cent of the total holding, with a maximum value of £20,000).
- Gains on the first disposal of Enterprise Investment Scheme shares.

Your home. Your main home is usually exempt from capital gains tax. However, there are certain 'ifs and buts' which could be important.

If you convert part of your home into an office or into self-contained accommodation on which you charge rent, that part of your home which is deemed to be a 'business' may be separately assessed – and CGT may be payable when you come to sell it. (CGT would not apply if you simply take in a lodger who is treated as family, in the sense of sharing your kitchen or bathroom.)

If you leave your home and let it for profit – perhaps because you have decided to live permanently with a friend – under tax law, the property would be treated as an investment and, subject to certain exemptions, would be assessed for CGT when it was sold.

Part of the argument hinges on owner occupation. If you are not living in the property (or a part of it which you have let out for rent), then the house – or that section of it – is no longer considered to be your main home. People who are liable for CGT in these circumstances can apply for special relief of up to £40,000.

If you leave your home to someone else who later decides to sell it, he/she may be liable for CGT when the property is sold (although only on the gain since the date of death). There may also be inheritance tax implications, so if you are thinking of leaving or giving your home to someone, you are strongly advised to consult a solicitor or accountant.

If you own two homes, only one of them is exempt from CGT, namely the one you designate as your 'main residence'.

Selling a family business. If you sell all or part of your business when you retire, you may not have to pay tax on the first £250,000 of capital gain with a further exemption allowed of one-half of gains between £250,000 and £1,000,000. To get maximum relief, you must be aged at least 50. If you are forced to retire early through ill health, the age rules may be applied less strictly and you may still be entitled to retirement relief.

There are also other possible tax benefits if you re-invest the profits within three years in another unquoted company.

Since this is a very complex field, before either retiring or selling shares, you are strongly recommended to seek professional advice.

Selling shares should not be confused with giving part of your family business to the next generation, which has been made easier under the inheritance tax rules. However, the advice about seeking professional help still applies.

Useful reading
For further information about capital gains tax, see the following booklets, available from any tax office:

- CGT 4 *Capital Gains Tax – Owner-Occupied Houses*
- CGT 6 *Capital Gains Tax – Retirement Disposal of A Business*
- CGT 11 *Capital Gains Tax and the Small Businessman*
- CGT 13 *The Indexation Allowance for Quoted Shares*
- CGT 14 *An Introduction to Capital Gains Tax*
- CGT 15 *Capital Gains Tax – A Guide for Married Couples*
- CGT 16 *Capital Gains Tax – Indexation Allowance*

Self-assessment

If you are one of the nine million people who needs to complete a tax return, you probably know that a new system of self-assessment was introduced at the start of the 1996-1997 tax year. It mainly affects the self-employed and higher rate taxpayers but could apply if part of your remuneration is not fully taxed under PAYE or if you have other income that is not fully taxed at source.

Self-assessment is optional. The aim is to simplify the process of making tax returns. However, rather than do it yourself, if you prefer you can leave it to the Revenue to work out the amount of tax you are due. There are penalties for late submissions, so it is important not to miss the critical dates. For further information, see leaflets IR 142 *Self Assessment – An Introduction* and *Self Assessment – A Guide for the Self-employed*, obtainable from any tax office.

Inheritance tax

Inheritance tax applies to money and/or gifts passed on at time of death (or sometimes before).

The first £215,000 of an individual's estate is tax free. Amounts over this are taxed at a single rate of 40 per cent. However, before any tax is calculated, there are a number of exemptions and other concessions of which perhaps the most important is that there is no tax on gifts or inheritance between spouses. Also, most family-owned businesses are exempted from inheritance tax; as are most life-time gifts, providing certain important conditions are met.

Gifts or money up to the value of £3,000 can be given annually free of tax, regardless of the particular date they were given.

Additionally, it is possible to make small gifts to any number of individuals free of tax, provided the amount to each does not exceed £250.

For exemption on other life-time gifts to apply, the gift must have been made at least seven years before the donor's death and, moreover, it must have been unconditionally given; or to use the jargon, 'without reservation'. A gift in which the donor retains an interest or some direct control – for example, a house 'given' to his children in which the parent continues to live – does not qualify for exemption.

The seven-year period is not totally inflexible, in that there is taper relief: in other words, a tapering rate of tax, according to how close to the seven year limit the death of the donor occurred. Gifts made within three years of death do not qualify for any relief and the tax will have to be paid in full.

For gifts made more than three years before death, the rates are as follows:

- Death between 3 and 4 years of gift, IHT reduced by 20%
- Death between 4 and 5 years of gift, IHT reduced by 40%
- Death between 5 and 6 years of gift, IHT reduced by 60%
- Death between 6 and 7 years of gift, IHT reduced by 80%

Quite apart from IHT, capital gains tax has to be paid on any gain that has built up on an asset you gave away during your lifetime and which is subsequently sold. The appreciation is only calculated from 1982 or subsequent year of purchase and any part of the asset's increased value due to inflation is not counted for tax. Moreover, tax specialists say that there are legitimate ways of minimising the liability. Since this is a fairly complex matter, professional advice is essential.

Another very important consideration is the need to make a will. Neglect to do so can have serious consequences for those whom you might wish to benefit. For further information, see 'Making a will' (page 179).

If you have already written a will, you are strongly recommended to have this checked by a professional adviser to ensure that you do not give money unnecessarily to the taxman.

For further information about inheritance tax, see booklets *An*

Introduction to Inheritance Tax (IHT 3), *Inheritance Tax on Lifetime Gifts* (IHT 2) and *Alterations to an Inheritance Following a Death* (IHT 8), obtainable from any tax office.

Expenditure taxes

Other than the duty on alcohol, tobacco and petrol, there are three main expenditure taxes: VAT, insurance premium tax, and air passenger duty.

VAT. You pay this automatically on most goods and services, at a flat rate of 17.5 per cent. N.B. Exceptionally, VAT on domestic fuel is only 8 per cent.

Insurance Premium Tax. Tax is 4 per cent and applies to premiums paid on all general insurance except travel insurance, if this is bought through a travel agent or tour operator – in which case the tax is 17.5 per cent. Travel insurance bought from other providers including insurance companies and brokers, is 4 per cent.

Air passenger duty. Passengers pay a £10 charge on flights within the UK and to other EC destinations. The charge is £20 on flights elsewhere.

UK pensions paid abroad

- Technically your State pension could be subject to income tax, as it derives from the UK. In practice, if this is your only source of UK income, tax would be unlikely to be charged.
- If you have an occupational pension, UK tax will normally be charged on the total of the two amounts.
- If the country where you are living has a double tax agreement with the UK, your income may be taxed there – and not in Britain. Britain now has a double tax agreement with most countries. For further information, check the position with your local tax office.
- If your pension is taxed in the UK, you will be able to claim part of your personal allowance as an offset. A married man living with his wife may also be able to claim part of the married couple's allowance.
- Both State and occupational pensions may be paid to any country. If you are planning to retire to Australia, Canada, New Zealand or Norway, you would be advised to check on the up-to-date position regarding any annual increases you

would expect to receive to your pension. Some people have found the level of their pension 'frozen' at the date they left Britain, while others have been liable for an unexpected tax overseas.

■ Any queries about your pension should be addressed to the DSS Overseas Benefits Directorate at Longbenton, Newcastle upon Tyne NE98 1YX.

5

Investment Wisdom

Investment is a subject for everyone. One of your most important aims must be to make your existing money work for you so you will be more comfortable in the years ahead.

Many articles on retirement planning concentrate almost exclusively on ways of boosting your immediate income to compensate for your loss of earnings. Frankly, this is very short-sighted. An equally if not even more critical concern must be to safeguard your long term security, even if this means some minor sacrifice to your current standard of living.

The likelihood is that you will live for 20 years or longer after you retire and your partner may live longer still. Your financial planning must therefore be aimed not just for your sixties but also for your eighties.

Inflation is another essential factor that must be taken into account since, unless you plan carefully, this could badly affect your standard of living after a few years.

Sources of investable funds

You do not need to be in the director league to have money for investment. Possible sources of quite significant capital include:

- Commuted lump sum from your pension
- Insurance policies, designed to mature around your retirement
- Profits on your home, if you sell it and move to smaller, less expensive accommodation
- Redundancy money, golden handshake or other farewell gift from your employer
- Sale of SAYE and other share option schemes.

General investment strategy

Investments differ in their aims, tax treatment and the amount of risk involved. Ideally you should plan to acquire a mix of investments, designed variously: to provide some income to supplement your pension and also some capital appreciation to maintain your standard of living long term.

Except for annuities and National Savings, which have sections to themselves, the different types of investment are listed by groups, as follows:

- Variable interest accounts
- Fixed interest securities
- Equities
- Long-term lock-ups.

As a general strategy, it is a good idea to aim to choose at least one type of investment from each group.

Annuities

Definition. A normal life annuity is a very simple investment to understand. You pay a capital sum to an insurance company and in return are guaranteed an income for life. The money is paid to you at fixed intervals and will remain exactly the same year in, year out. Payments are calculated according to life expectancy tables and for this reason an annuity is not really a suitable investment for anyone under 70. Other than your age, the key factor affecting payments is the level of interest rates at the time you buy: the higher these are, the more you will receive.

An annuity would probably give you more immediate income than any other form of investment. But whether you actually get good value depends on how long you live. When you die, your capital will be gone. So if you die a short while after signing the contract, it will represent very bad value indeed. On the other hand, if you live a very long time, you may more than recoup your original capital.

As a precaution against early death, it is possible to take out a capital protected annuity, i.e. one guaranteed for a specified number of years. Should you die before the end of the contract, the payments will go to your partner or other beneficiary. The big drawback is that if you outlive the contract, you will not get any more annuity income.

There are also other types of annuity, such as capital and income plans which pay you a small income, say, for a 10-year period, at the end of which your capital is returned.

Annuities, such as those described above, which you choose to buy as a purely optional purchase should not be confused with **pension-linked annuities** which are a required purchase for people with personal pensions or with other types of money purchase plans. For further information about compulsory purchase annuities, see page 35.

Tax. Income tax on optional annuities is relatively low, as part of the income is allowed as a return on capital which is not taxable. Pension-linked annuities are fully taxable.

How to obtain. You can buy an annuity either direct from an insurance company or via an intermediary, such as an independent financial adviser (IFA). But shop around, as the payments vary considerably. For names of IFAs, contact: **IFA Promotion Ltd.**, T:0117 971 1177; **IFA Association**, T:0171 240 7878.

Assessment. Safe. Attractive if you live to a ripe old age. But highly vulnerable to inflation. Sacrifice of capital that might otherwise benefit successors.

National savings

It is very easy to invest in National Savings, as all you need do is go to the post office for information or telephone the National Savings Sales Information Unit on T:0645 645000 (Monday – Friday, 8.30 a.m. to 5 p.m.); all calls are charged at local rates.

Most types of investment offered by NS are broadly similar to those provided by banks and other financial institutions. So rather than explain in detail the exact terms and conditions of, say, a National Savings Investment Account, it is easier to suggest that you pick up the relevant leaflet at the post office counter or telephone the above number.

The main investments offered by National Savings are:

■ **Ordinary account.** Pays a fairly low rate of variable interest. You can invest between £10 and £10,000. The first £70 of interest each year is free of tax. Ask for booklet DNS 760.

■ **Investment account.** Pays an attractive rate of interest. You can invest between £20 and £100,000. Interest is taxable but paid in full without deduction of tax at source. Ask for booklet DNS 761.

■ **Income bonds.** Pay attractive rate of interest. Interest which is taxable is paid gross. You can invest between £2,000 and £250,000. Ask for booklet DNS 767.

■ **National Savings Certificates.** Offer an attractive rate of fixed interest that is tax free. You can invest from £100 to £10,000. For maximum benefit, you must hold the certificates for five years. Ask for booklet DNS 762.

■ **Index-linked certificates.** You can invest from £100 to £10,000. You get interest (at time of writing 2.5 per cent) plus the increase in the Retail Prices Index. To get the best return, certificates must be kept for five years. Interest is tax free. Ask for booklet DNS 763.

■ **Gilts.** Can be bought through the National Savings Stock Register (NSSR). Ask for booklet DNS 766.

■ **Capital bonds.** These offer a guaranteed interest rate, providing you do not withdraw your money before five years. The one big drawback is that tax on the interest has to be paid annually – with higher bills every year as the interest grows – until you actually receive any money. Minimum purchase is £100. Ask for booklet DNS 768.

■ **Children's Bonus Bond.** Bonds are sold in multiples of £25 and the maximum purchase per child in the current issue is £1,000. Both interest and bonus, which will be paid after five years, are free of income tax. Interested parents and grandparents should ask for booklet DNS 769.

■ **First Option Bond.** Guaranteed growth bond, offering a 12-month fixed rate of interest provided the money is not withdrawn earlier. You can invest between £1,000 and £250,000. Ask for booklet DNS 770.

■ **Pensioners Guaranteed Income Bond.** A special bond for savers aged over 60, offering a guaranteed rate of interest for five years. The income which is taxable is paid monthly. Minimum purchase is £500; the maximum, £50,000. Ask for booklet DNS 773.

Variable interest accounts

Few people who rely on interest from their savings to provide them with extra income in their retirement will need reminding that interest rates can go down as well as up! This is not a reason for forgetting all about variable interest accounts (when interest rates were high, they provided one of the best homes for many people's money); but it is essential to understand how such accounts work – together with their advantages and drawbacks.

Recent changes. Most banks and building societies have introduced interest bearing current accounts. Although an improvement on the standard current account, these are not suitable for keeping large savings for more than a short time. If you are tempted to switch to an interest bearing account, check what charges apply if you dip into overdraft. You should also enquire whether you are being offered 'tiered rates' – those paying the top rate of interest applicable on all your funds; or the less attractive 'banded rates' – those with two levels of interest, with a lower amount paid on, say, the first £500 or £1,000 and the higher rate only on funds above that amount.

A further point to investigate is whether there is a fixed monthly or other charge. This can sometimes change without customers being properly informed.

Definition. Other than the interest bearing accounts described above, these are all deposit accounts (share accounts in building societies) of one form or another, arranged with banks, building societies and the National Savings Bank. They include among others: basic deposit accounts, high interest accounts and fixed term deposit accounts; and also TESSAs.

Your money collects interest while it is on deposit, which may be credited to your account or for which you may receive a regular cheque. Some institutions pay interest annually; others pay monthly. If you have a preference, this is a point to check. The rate of interest will vary, up or down, according to the level of national interest rates. While you may get a poor return on your money if interest rates drop, your savings will nearly always be safe as you are not taking any kind of investment risk.

Access. This depends on the type of account you choose: you may have a cheque book and withdraw your money when you want; you may have to give about a week's notice; or if you enter into a term account, you will have to leave your money deposited for the specified period. In general, accounts where a longer period of notice is required earn a better rate of interest.

Sum deposited. It is not usually sensible to consider a deposit account unless you have a minimum of £100. For certain types of account, the minimum investment could be anything from £500 to about £5,000.

Tax. With the exception both of TESSAs, which are tax-free, and of the National Savings Bank, where interest is paid gross, tax is deducted at source – so you can spend the money without worrying about tax. However, you must enter the interest on your tax return; and if you are a higher rate taxpayer, you will have additional liability.

Non-taxpayers can arrange to have their interest paid in full by completing a certificate which enables the financial institution to pay the interest gross.

Choosing a deposit account

There are two key choices: the type of deposit account you want and where to invest your money. The basic points to consider are as follows:

Basic deposit account. This attracts a relatively low rate of interest. But it is both easy to set up and very flexible, as you can add savings when you like and can usually withdraw your money without any notice. It is a much better option than simply leaving your money in a current account and is a good temporary home for your cash if you are saving short-term for, say, a holiday. However, it is not recommended as a long-term savings plan.

High interest deposit account. Your money earns a higher rate of interest than it would on an ordinary deposit account. You will need to deposit a minimum sum, which could be around £500 to £1,000. While you can always add to this amount, if your basic deposit drops below the required minimum, your money will stop earning the higher interest rate.

Fixed term deposit account. You deposit your money for an agreed period of time, variously from a few months to over a year. In return, you will be paid a relatively star rate of interest.

There is a minimum investment of roughly £1,500 to £5,000. If you need to withdraw your money before the end of the agreed term, there are usually hefty penalties. Before entering into a term account, you need to be sure that you can afford to leave the money on deposit.

You will also need to take a view about interest rates: if they are generally low, your money may be better invested elsewhere.

It is important to keep a note of the date when the agreement expires. As a rule, your money will no longer earn preferential rates after the term has ended. The bank or other institution may not notify you in advance and may, quite legitimately, simply credit you with the normal interest rates after the contract's expiry.

Tax Exempt Special Savings Account (TESSA). TESSAs are special deposit accounts which, provided you leave the savings in the account for the five years the scheme lasts, allow you to keep all interest tax free.

The maximum you are allowed to invest is £9,000. This can either be paid in regular monthly amounts, of up to £150; or in annual sums, as follows: year one, a maximum of £3,000; years two, three and four, up to £1,800 each year; year five, up to £600.

The capital (i.e. your savings in the TESSA) cannot be withdrawn until the end of year five, otherwise you lose the tax advantage. People who need some money can, however, withdraw part of the interest less basic rate tax.

For most taxpayers who can afford to save for five years, TESSAs are an attractive investment. But remember, interest rates vary from one bank and building society to another, so the usual advice about shopping around applies.

N.B. People with an existing TESSA can, once it matures, invest all the savings from their first TESSA – excluding any interest – into a new scheme. £9,000 is still the maximum allowed.

Fixed interest securities

In contrast to variable interest accounts, fixed interest securities offer a fixed rate of interest which you are paid, whatever happens to interest rates generally. Since most are only suitable for those who can afford riskier investments, we only describe gilts as these are guaranteed by the government.

Gilt-edged securities

Definition. These are stocks which guarantee both the interest payable and the repayment price promised on a given date.

The maturity date can be anything from a few months to 20 years or longer. Stocks are variously known as: short-dated, medium-dated and long-dated. A further category is undated. Additionally, there are index-linked gilts.

Prices are quoted per £100 of nominal stock. For example, a stock may be quoted as: 10 per cent Treasury Stock 1999, 99 1/2 – 100 1/4. In plain English, this means the following:

■ 10 per cent represents the interest you will be paid. You will receive the interest payment twice yearly, 5 per cent each time.
■ You are buying Treasury Stock.
■ The maturity date is 1999.
■ To buy the stock, you will have to pay £100.25p (i.e.100 1/4).
■ If you want to sell, the market price you will get is £99.50p (i.e. 99 1/2).

Gilts are complicated by the fact that you can either retain them until their maturity date, in which case the government will return the nominal value in full. Or you can sell them on the Stock Exchange at market value.

Prices are affected by current interest rates. If interest rates are at 7 per cent, a gilt with a guaranteed interest payment of 10 per cent is a very attractive buy – so the price will rise. Conversely, if interest rates are 15 per cent, a guaranteed interest payment of 10 per cent is a poor proposition, so the price will drop.

Index-linked Gilts are designed to shield investors against inflation: they pay very low interest but are redeemable at a higher price than the initial purchase price, as their value is geared to the cost of living. They are most valuable when inflation is high.

Tax. Income tax is normally deducted at source. However, if you buy gilts on the National Savings Stock Register (NSSR), the interest will be paid to you gross. This does not mean that you avoid paying it, simply that you must allow for a future tax bill before spending the money.

A particular attraction of gilts is that they are free of capital gains tax.

How to buy. You can buy gilts through banks, building societies, a stockbroker, financial intermediary or through National Savings. In all cases, you will be charged commission. A booklet *Government Stock – Buy Gilts Without A Stockbroker* is available from most post offices.

Assessment. Gilts normally pay reasonably good interest and offer excellent security, in that they are backed by the government. You can sell at very short notice and the stock is normally accepted by banks as security for loans, if you want to run an overdraft.

However, gilts are not a game for amateurs as, if you buy or sell at the wrong time, you could lose money; and if you hold your stock to redemption, inflation could take its toll on your investment.

Gilt plans. This is a technique for linking the purchase of gilt-edged securities and with-profit life insurance policies to provide security of capital and income over a 10 to 20-year period. These plans are normally obtainable from financial intermediaries.

Equities

These are all stocks and shares, involving varying degrees of risk. They are designed to achieve capital appreciation as well as give you some regular income. They are easy to purchase thanks to the increase in telephone share-dealing facilities. Most allow you to get your money out within thirty days or less.

Equities can be excellent money-spinners but there is always some risk. They include: ordinary shares, unit trusts and personal equity plans.

Ordinary shares listed on the Stock Exchange

Definition. Public companies issue shares as a way of raising money. When you buy shares and become a shareholder, you participate in the profits through a dividend. In bad years, it is possible that no dividends will be paid. In good years, dividends can increase substantially.

The money you invest is unsecured. This means that, quite apart from any dividends, your capital could be slashed in value – or if the company goes bankrupt, you could lose the lot. Against this, if the company performs well you could greatly increase your wealth.

You can buy shares via a stockbroker, a share shop, the securities department of your bank or use a telephone share dealing service. In all cases, you will be charged commission and stamp duty. You will be issued with a share certificate which you or your adviser must keep, as you will have to produce it when you wish to sell.

You may be advised to use a nominee account, as being cheaper and more convenient. The one big disadvantage is that you may miss out on access to various benefits – including shareholders' perks.

Tax. If your total profits in the year from selling shares exceed £6,500, you could be liable for capital gains tax.

Unit trusts

Definition. Your money is pooled in a fund, run by managers, who invest the proceeds in a wide range of shares and other securities. The advantages are: it is usually less risky, it is very simple and you get professional management. Also, every trust is required by law to have a trustee to protect investors' interests.

The minimum investment in some of the more popular trusts is £500; in others, it can be as high as £10,000. Some trusts allow you to purchase units for smaller amounts on a regular monthly plan.

There is often a front end fee of around 5 per cent to join the trust and also an annual management charge.

All unit holders receive an income distribution – normally paid every six months. You can sell all or part of your investment by telling the unit trust managers that you wish to do so.

How to obtain. Units are purchased from the management companies, which can be: banks, building societies, insurance companies, stockbrokers, financial intermediaries or specialist unit trust management groups.

For a list of unit trusts and other information contact the **Unit Trust Information Service**, 65 Kingsway, London WC2B 6TD. T:0181 207 1361.

Tax. PEP unit trusts have special advantages. Otherwise tax treatment is identical to ordinary shares.

Assessment. An ideal method for smaller investors to buy stocks and shares: both less risky and easier.

Open-Ended Investment Companies (OEICs). These are a new type of fund which, because they are expected to be cheaper, more flexible and easier to understand, are expected in the long term to replace unit trusts. A factsheet explaining OEICs in more detail is available free from the **Association of Unit Trusts and Investment Funds**. T:0181 207 1361.

Investment Trusts are companies that invest in the shares of other companies, providing a spread of risk. You can buy investment trusts through a saving and investment scheme which is simple and cheap. Split capital trusts separate capital growth and income growth. These can be mixed and matched to meet your needs during retirement.

For a free information pack, write to **The Association of Investment Trust Companies,** Durrant House, 8-13 Chiswell Street, London EC1Y 4YY.

Personal equity plan

PEPs allow you to buy shares in a range of investments including corporate bonds and investment trusts, with the advantage that all income and gains are exempt from tax.

The maximum you can invest a year is £9,000: £6,000 in a general PEP plus £3,000 in a single company PEP. If you acquire shares in your company's 'all employee share scheme', you can transfer up to £3,000 worth into a single company PEP in any one year.

Equally, if you receive shares as a result of a building society or insurance business demutualisation, these too can be transferred into a PEP provided you make the transaction within 42 days.

The money has to be invested through an authorised manager, for example: a bank, building society or financial intermediary.

Tax. PEPS are free of both income tax and capital gains tax.

Assessment. The inclusion of (lower risk) corporate bonds among the list of eligible investments could have appeal for more cautious investors. The tax advantages are attractive. But no shares are without risk. Also some PEP managers charge pretty hefty fees. Investigate carefully before deciding.

Long-term lock-ups

Certain types of investment, mostly offered by insurance companies, provide fairly high guaranteed growth in exchange for your undertaking to leave a lump sum with them or to pay regular premiums for a fixed period, probably 10 years. Many are linked with some form of life assurance cover.

Life assurance policies

Definition. Life assurance can provide your successors with money when you die; or it can be used as a savings plan to provide you with a lump sum on a fixed date.

There are three basic types of life assurance: whole life policies, term policies and endowment policies.

Whole life policies are designed to pay out on death. In its most straightforward form, the scheme works as follows: you pay a premium every year and, when you die, your beneficiaries receive the money.

As with an ordinary household policy, the insurance only holds good if you continue the payments. If one year you did not pay and were to die, the policy could be void and your successors would receive nothing.

Term policies involve a definite commitment, i.e.: you elect to make regular payments for an agreed period, say ten years. If you die during this period, your family will be paid the agreed sum in full.

It is possible to arrange for the benefit to be paid out as regular income. This is known as **family income benefit**. The payments will cease at the end of the insured term. If you die after the end of the term, your family will normally receive nothing.

Many people argue that such policies, while eminently sensible when children are growing up, are one expense that can cheerfully be dropped on retirement. This could be short-sighted. A big problem for many widows is that, when their husband dies, part of his pension dies with him. A lump sum or regular income plan could make all the difference in helping to bridge the gap. Alternatively – and for many this is a more attractive option – whole life or term can be converted into an endowment policy.

Endowment policies are essentially a savings plan. You contract to pay regular premiums over 10 or 25 years and receive a lump sum at the end.

Once you have committed yourself, you have to go on paying every year, as there are heavy penalties if you stop. This is especially true during the early years. The terms should be clearly spelt out on the sales literature.

An important feature of endowment policies is that if you die before the policy matures, the remaining payments are excused and your successors will be paid a lump sum on your death.

Endowment policies are a very popular way of making extra financial provision for retirement. The amount of money you stand to receive can vary hugely, however, depending on the charges. Aim to compare at least three policies before choosing.

Options. Both whole life policies and endowment policies offer two basic options: with profits or without profits. Very briefly the difference is as follows:

Without profits. This is sometimes known as 'guaranteed sum assured'. It means that the insurance company guarantees you a specific fixed sum which you know in advance and is what you – or your successors – will be paid.

With profits. You are paid a guaranteed fixed sum plus an addition, based on the profits that the insurance company has made by investing your payments. The basic premiums are higher and the profits element is not known in advance. If the insurance company has invested your money wisely, a 'with profits' policy provides a useful hedge against inflation. If its investment policy is mediocre, you could have paid higher premiums for very little extra return.

Unit linked. This is a refinement of the 'with profits' policy, in that the investment element of the policy is linked in with a unit trust.

Other basics. Premiums can normally be paid monthly or annually. Size of premium varies, depending on: the type of policy you choose and the amount of cover you want. As very general guidance, £35-£40 a month would probably be a normal starting figure. Higher premiums often give better value as relatively less of your contribution is swallowed up in administrative costs.

Most policies require you to sign a declaration of health. It is very important that this should be honestly completed: if you make a claim and it is discovered that you gave misleading information, the insurance company could refuse to pay.

How to obtain. Policies are available through banks, insurance companies, independent financial advisers (IFAs) and building societies. The biggest problem for most people is the enormous choice. Another difficulty can be understanding the small print: terms which sound very similar may obscure important differences which could affect your benefit.

It is usually advisable to consult an IFA, who should give you full details of the risks, benefits, charges and his/her reasons for recommending a particular policy. For a list of local IFAs, contact: **IFA Promotion Ltd.**, 17-19 Emery Road, Brislington, Bristol BS4 5JJ. T:0117 971 1177; **IFA Association**, 12-13 Henrietta Street, London WC2E 8LH. T:0171 240 7878. See also 'Where to go for Financial Advice', page 88.

The **Association of British Insurers (ABI)** has a number of useful booklets on life assurance. Contact ABI, 51 Gresham Street, London EC2V 7HQ.

Tax. The proceeds of a qualifying policy – whether taken as a lump sum or in regular income payments (as in the case of family income benefit) – are free of all tax.

Assessment. Life assurance is normally a sensible investment, whether the aim is to provide death cover or the benefits of a lump sum to boost your retirement income. It is very attractive from a tax angle. Also, certain policies provide good capital appreciation (although recent bonuses have tended to be disappointing). However, you are locked into a long term commitment. So, choosing the right policy is very important. Shop around, take advice and, above all, do not sign anything unless you are absolutely certain that you understand every word.

Alternatives to surrendering a policy

As already mentioned, there are heavy penalties if you surrender an endowment policy before its maturity. Some people, either because they can no longer afford the payments or for some other reason, wish to terminate the agreement – regardless of any losses they may make/or investment gains they sacrifice.

Instead of simply surrendering the policy, people in this situation have two alternative options, both of which stand to yield them a higher return than surrender. The one is to sell the policy by auction; the other to sell it outright.

Auctioneers typically charge a registration fee (about £50) plus commission on the excess (they make at auction) above the surrender value quoted. The risk is minimal, since if the policy fails to reach its reserve it can still be surrendered in the normal way.

Market makers who buy policies offer a cash price that at the very least would be higher than the surrender value. To be of interest to them, the policy would need to meet their purchasing criteria, e.g. age of policy and length of time to maturity.

A full list of dealers that buy and sell mid-term policies is obtainable from the **Association of Policy Market Makers.** T:0171 739 3949.

Investor protection

Anyone selling investment products, or policies, must by law be authorised by a regulatory body, all of which have strict rules. For your protection, there are a number of essentials you should know.

■ Never deal with any adviser without knowing by whom they are authorised. The most likely body is the PIA but could be IMRO, SFA or SIB.

■ Businesses may either promote their own in-house investment plans (unit trusts, insurance policies and so on) or they must act as independent consultants and have no vested interest in any product they recommend. Make sure you know which your adviser is.

■ To give 'best advice', independent consultants need to understand your requirements in detail. Before asking you to sign, they should give you a 'reason why' letter explaining why they believe their recommendation best meets your needs.

■ Some advisers charge fees for their time. Some are paid in commission. Others receive a salary with commission on top. You are at perfect liberty to ask which applies and to enquire what the commission level is.

■ All charges including management fees should be clearly stated on the literature. Make sure before signing that you understand the total amount you will have to pay.

Complaints

If you have a complaint, you should take it up with the firm, or adviser, concerned. If this gets nowhere, approach the relevant ombudsman or referee (the regulatory body will advise you). In most cases this will be the PIA Ombudsman.

He handles complaints about PIA member firms, namely: unit trusts, life companies (including life assurance arms of banks and building societies), fund management companies and independent financial advisers. The list includes insurance salesmen and others selling personal pensions. If he thinks your complaint is justified, he can order compensation.

For further information, contact: **The PIA Ombudsman Bureau,** Hertsmere House, Hertsmere Road, London E14 4AB. T:0171 216 0016.

6

Where to go for Financial Advice

When thinking about retirement planning, it is important to get as much advice as possible. Even if you have never done so before, there is no cause to feel hesitant about approaching financial advisers.

As someone who may shortly be retiring, you are seen as a very attractive potential client, especially if you are a member of a pension scheme with a sizeable commuted lump sum to invest.

Before making contact, it is generally a good idea to try to sort out your priorities, for example: whether you are looking for capital growth or whether your main objective is to increase your income. Also, if you have any special plans such as helping your grandchildren or spending money on home improvements, these too should be thought through in advance as they could affect the advice you receive.

Another reason for doing some advance thinking is that, whereas some advisers – for example, insurance brokers – do not specifically charge you for their time, others such as accountants and solicitors charge fees by the hour. Drinking coffee in their office and musing about the future delights of retirement may be a pleasant way of spending the afternoon but it can also work out to be pretty costly!

Choosing an adviser

When choosing an adviser, there are usually four main considerations: respectability, suitability, price and convenience.

Where your money is concerned, you cannot afford to take unnecessary risks. Merely establishing that an individual is a member of a recognised institution, while a basic safeguard, is insufficient recommendation if you want to be assured of dealing with someone who will personally suit you. The principle applies as much with friends, as with complete strangers.

If you are thinking of using an adviser whom you do not already know in a professional capacity, you should certainly check on their reputation and, ideally, talk to some of their clients. No one who is any good will object to your asking for references.

Also, quite apart from general competence, professional help is very much a question of 'horses for courses'. Just as you would hardly consult a divorce lawyer if you were buying a house, so too in the financial field most practitioners have different areas of expertise. It is, therefore, important to establish that your adviser has the particular capability you require.

It generally makes sense to choose a firm that is reasonably accessible. If you live in a part of the country where the choice of financial advisers is limited, you can approach one of the organisations listed on the following pages that maintain a register of members – or, you could ask your bank manager to recommend someone suitable.

Finally, you should be aware that some specialist advisers earn commission, so have a vested interest in any sale they make. Also some brokers and dealers are tied agents for a specific company so can only promote their own in-house products. To know where you stand, you should ask any agent whom he represents; whether he is a tied agent; and why in particular he is recommending X product, or policy, as being most suitable for you.

Accountants

Accountants are specialists in matters to do with taxation. They can help you avoid paying more tax than you need and can assess the tax effects of different types of investment you may be considering. Likewise, they can help you with charitable covenants, the preparation of tax returns and if you are thinking of becoming self-employed, they will be able to assist you with some of the practicalities – such as registering for VAT and establishing a system of business accounts.

If you need help in finding a suitable accountant, any of the following should be able to assist:

Institute of Chartered Accountants in England and Wales, PO Box 433, Chartered Accountants' Hall, Moorgate Place, London EC2P 2BJ.

Institute of Chartered Accountants of Scotland, 27 Queen Street, Edinburgh EH2 1LA.

Institute of Chartered Accountants in Ireland, Chartered Accountants House, 87-89 Pembroke Road, Dublin 4.

Association of Chartered Certified Accountants, 29 Lincoln's Inn Fields, London WC2A 3EE.

Complaints. Anyone with a complaint against an accountant can write to the Secretary of the Institute's Investigating Committee who, if the complaint is valid, will refer the matter to the Disciplinary Committee.

Banks

Most people need no introduction to the clearing banks since, if they have a bank account, they have probably been popping in and out of their local branch for years.

Yet despite the fact that the counter is usually well decorated with leaflets, many customers do not actually realise what a comprehensive service their bank provides.

In addition to the normal account facilities, all the major high street banks offer investment, insurance and tax planning services, as well as advice on drawing up a will.

Barclays Bank Plc, 54 Lombard Street, London EC3P 3AH. Offers customers a range of accounts to suit a variety of personal savings requirements. Their financial planning services (available through subsidiary companies) include: personal investment advice, investment management, stockbroking, unit trusts, life assurance, pensions, personal taxation, wills and trusts.

You can either write to the above address or apply through your local branch.

Lloyds Bank Plc, 71 Lombard Street, London EC3P 3BS. The Lloyds Bank Classic account offers all the normal facilities of a current account plus interest on credit balances.

Lloyds Private Banking Ltd., Capital House, 1-5 Perrymount Road, Haywards Heath, West Sussex RH16 3SP provides independent advice on the whole spectrum of investments including assistance with taxation, wills and estate planning.

Other facilities include: a Unit Trust Management Service, a PEP Centre and an Insurance Services company.

Midland Financial Services (Division of Midland Bank plc), Poultry, London EC2P 2BX. Offers a range of stockbroking and personal financial services. There is a comprehensive choice of financial products including unit trusts, PEPs and life assurance, which are selected according to a customer's requirements by a personal financial planning manager.

Midland also offers an Estate Planning Service which includes preparation of a will, drawing up trusts and administering customers' estates.

Any Midland branch can arrange a meeting if you would like to discuss these services.

National Westminster Bank Plc, 41 Lothbury, London EC2P 2BP. Offers a full range of banking services including financial planning for retirement. A meeting with a NatWest adviser can be arranged free of charge. To make an appointment, contact your local NatWest branch or call free on 0800 200400.

Royal Bank of Scotland, 42 St Andrew Square, Edinburgh EH2 2YE. Offers a choice of three interest paying accounts. The Bank's Private Trust and Taxation Department gives free advice on making a will, although the usual legal fees apply if you proceed; write to The Royal Bank of Scotland, Freepost, PO Box 31, Edinburgh EH2 0BG.

The Bank also offers a personal tax service with work charged according to its complexity.

Investment management services are provided through Newton Management and Royal Scottish Assurance; information can be obtained from any branch of the Bank.

Abbey National Plc, 215-229 Baker Street, London NW1 6XL. Offers a range of savings, mortgage, pension, current account and insurance products; and also loans for such items as home improvements, or to finance a holiday. There are various savings accounts paying tiered rates of interest including an instant access account that can be opened with £50, as well as TESSAs, PEPs, Bonds and other accounts.

Additionally, Abbey National IFA (at 77 Gracechurch Street, London EC3V 0DL. T:0171 548 1400) offers independent financial planning for those nearing retirement or facing redundancy.

Full details of all Abbey National services can be obtained from any high street branch; or call T:0800 555100.

New high street banks. During 1997, several building societies have converted to banks. By time of publication, these were expected to include: The Halifax, Woolwich, Alliance & Leicester, Bristol &

West – with Northern Rock planned to convert during the autumn. Full information about their services should be obtainable from your local branch.

Complaints

The Banking Ombudsman acts as an independent arbitrator, who aims to resolve complaints by individuals and small businesses about banking services from the 52 banks (and designated associates) which come within the scheme. These include all the main high street banks. His decisions are binding and he is empowered to award compensation of up to £100,000. The service is free.

Complaints can be handled on most aspects of personal banking, including bank credit cards, as well as maladministration or undue delays in dealing with wills and trusts. However, except where there has been maladministration, the Ombudsman's powers do not extend to commercial decisions on the grant of an overdraft or loan.

The address to which to write is: **The Banking Ombudsman**, 70 Gray's Inn Road, London WC1X 8NB. T:0171 404 9944.

Insurance sales people

The insurance business covers a very wide range from straightforward policies – such as motor or household insurance – to the rather more complex areas, including life assurance and pensions. Quite apart from the confusion of the enormous choice of policies and the importance of ensuring that you understand the conditions laid down in the small print, a further difficulty is the number of different categories of people – agents, salesmen, brokers, independent financial advisers (IFAs) – who may try to sell you insurance.

Insurance brokers

Unless you are already dealing with an insurance company that suits you, you would normally consult an insurance broker for advice about the more everyday type of insurance, e.g. motor, medical, household and holiday insurance.

A broker should be able to help you choose the most suitable policies, help you determine how much cover you require and explain any technical terms contained in the documents. He can also assist with any claims and advise you when renewals are necessary. An essential point to check before proceeding is that the firm the broker represents is registered with the Insurance Brokers Registration Council.

Although a condition of registration is that a broker must deal with many insurers and therefore be in a position to offer a wide choice of policies, most companies pay insurance brokers on a commission basis; so, it is possible that you could be offered advice that is not totally unbiased.

Generally speaking, you are safer to use a larger brokerage with an established reputation. Also, before you take out a policy, it is advisable to consult several brokers in order to get a better feel for the market. **The British Insurance and Investment Brokers Association** (BIIBA House, 14 Bevis Marks, London EC3A 7NT) can send you a list of brokers in your area.

Complaints. If you have a complaint against a registered insurance broker you could contact the Insurance Brokers Registration Council. They will investigate the matter and, if they think your complaint is justified, will seek to get redress for you. You should write to the Registrar at: **Insurance Brokers Registration Council**, 63 St. Mary Ave, London EC3A 8NB. T:0171 621 1061.

Another useful source is the Association of British Insurers, which represents over 430 companies, who between them handle about 90 per cent of business done by British insurance companies. If you are in dispute with one of the Association's members, the ABI will ensure that your complaint is dealt with at top level. The address is: **Association of British Insurers (ABI)**, 51 Gresham Street, London EC2V 7HQ. T:0171 600 3333.

There is also an **Insurance Ombudsman.** He exists to help private policy holders only and cannot take up the cudgels on behalf of commercial organisations. The company in question must be a member of the Ombudsman Scheme. You can find this out from your insurance company, broker, a CAB or from the Ombudsman's Bureau direct. Thirdly, you must contact the Ombudsman within six months of the insurance company's final decision on the dispute.

The Ombudsman has power to make awards up to £100,000 and while he can adjudicate on most issues, some matters such as third party claims are outside his scope. He will also not be able to help if legal proceedings have been started.

For further information, contact: **The Insurance Ombudsman Bureau**, City Gate One, 135 Park Street, London SE1 9EA. T:0171 928 7600.

Independent financial advisers (IFAs)

IFAs specialise in advising on products and policies with some investment content including, for example, endowment policies, life assurance and unit trusts.

They help you work out what type of policy would be most suitable for you and where you could obtain best value for money. They can also handle all the arrangements for you.

Before committing yourself, you should ask your adviser a number of questions, including: by whom they are regulated; what charges are involved; what commission, if any, he/she will be getting; whether it is possible you could lose money; how soon surrender values will equal premiums paid; and why, in particular, you are being recommended to buy the policy or investment in question. Your adviser should provide you with both a 'key features document' and a 'reason why letter', answering all these points. It is essential to read them carefully and if there is anything you do not understand, you should certainly ask!

While commission is still the norm, some financial advisers now offer a fee-based service, rather in the manner of an accountant or solicitor. This means, of course, that clients are charged an up-front fee. But against this, they are not forfeiting the often very much larger sum – deducted from their investment – that the IFA would have received. Because of the way some insurance companies operate, fee-charging advisers may still receive the commission in the first instance but will then – depending on the client's preference – either rebate it back to them in cash or (and this could be more sensible) re-invest it on their behalf in the product.

Local names and addresses of IFAs can be obtained from any of the following:

The Money Management National Register of Fee-based Advisers, Freepost 22 (SW1565), London W1E 7EZ. T:0117 976 9444 (enclose sae).

IFA Promotion Ltd., 17-19 Emery Road, Brislington, Bristol BS4 5JJ. T:0117 971 1177.

IFA Association, 12-13 Henrietta Street, London WC2E 8LH. T:0171 240 7878.

Complaints

If you have a complaint about an IFA, the most likely person to be able to help is the PIA Ombudsman.

Before approaching him, you must first try to settle the dispute with the company or adviser direct. If this fails, the Ombudsman will investigate your complaint and if he finds it justified can award compensation. Although he has very wide powers, the Ombudsman cannot intervene over an actuarial dispute. Nor will he be able to assist if legal proceedings have been started.

For further information, write to the **PIA Ombudsman Bureau,** Hertsmere House, Hertsmere Road, London E14 4AB. T:0171 216 0016.

Solicitors

Solicitors are professional advisers on subjects to do with the law or on matters that could have legal implications. They can assist with: the purchase or rental of property; drawing up a will; if you are charged with a criminal offence; or if you are sued in a civil matter.

Additionally, their advice can be invaluable in vetting any important document before you sign it. A solicitor can also help with the legal formalities of setting up a business; trusts; guardianship arrangements or other agreement, where the intention is to make it binding. Likewise, a solicitor would normally be the first person to consult if you were thinking of suing an individual or commercial organisation.

If you need to find a solicitor, often the best way is through recommendation. Your bank manager or accountant should be able to advise.

Another solution is to consult the *Solicitors' and Barristers' Directory and Diary,* available in public libraries and CABs, which lists the names and addresses of solicitors all over the country, together with brief details about the type of work in which they have experience.

If you need financial as well as legal help, you could contact SIFA (Solicitors for Independent Financial Advice) which will send you details of up to six local firms able to advise about such matters as pension planning, investments or choosing a long term care policy. The address is: SIFA, 10 East Street, Epsom, Surrey KT17 1HH. T:01372 721172.

If you want information about your rights, you could approach a Law Centre. The advice is free. You can get the address from the town hall or CAB. Or you can contact **Law Centres Federation,** Duchess House, 18-19 Warren Street, London W1P 5DB. T:0171 387 8570.

Legal Aid

If you need a legal aid solicitor (or want to find out if you are eligible for legal aid), the place to go is your Citizens' Advice Bureau. If you are entitled to legal aid, your CAB will explain what is involved and can help you find a solicitor. Alternatively, you could contact the **Legal Aid Board**, Press and Public Relations Section, 85 Gray's Inn Road, London WC1X 8AA. T:0171 813 1000.

Complaints

If you have a complaint against a solicitor, The Office for the Supervision of Solicitors may be able to help. It can investigate such complaints as: failure to reply to letters; delay in dealing with your case; overcharging; wrongly retaining your papers; dishonesty and deception. It can also deal with complaints which allege 'inadequate professional service' (IPS) and is able to award compensation up to £1,000.

The Office cannot, however, give legal advice or tell a solicitor how to handle a case; nor can it investigate claims of professional negligence. The difference between inadequate professional service (IPS) and negligence is that IPS is substandard work, whereas negligence is a mistake by your solicitor which has lost you money or caused some other loss for which you may be entitled to financial redress.

If you believe you have a complaint of negligence, the Office for the Supervision of Solicitors will either put you in touch with a solicitor specialising in negligence claims or pass your complaint to the Solicitors Indemnity Fund (which deals with insurance claims). If an appointment for you is arranged with a solicitor, he/she will see you free of charge for up to an hour.

For further information contact: **The Office for the Supervision of Solicitors,** Victoria Court, 8 Dormer Place, Leamington Spa CV32 5AE. T:01926 820082.

If you are still not satisfied, you can approach the **Legal Services Ombudsman** at 22 Oxford Court, Oxford Street, Manchester M2 3WQ. T:0161 236 9532.

General queries. For queries of a more general nature, you should approach: **The Law Society,** 113 Chancery Lane, London WC2A 1PL. T:0171 242 1222.

For those in Scotland and Northern Ireland. If you live in Scotland or Northern Ireland, The Office for the Supervision of Solicitors will not be able to help you. Instead contact the Law Society at the relevant address below:

The Law Society of Scotland, The Law Society's Hall, 26-28 Drumsheugh Gardens, Edinburgh EH3 7YR. T:0131 226 7411.

The Law Society of Northern Ireland, Law Society House, 98 Victoria Street, Belfast BT1 3JZ. T:01232 231614.

7

Home Decisions

One of the most important decisions to be taken as you approach retirement is where you will live. To many people, one of the biggest attractions is the pleasure of moving home. No longer tied to an area within easy commuting distance of work, they can indulge their dreams of a cottage in the Cotswolds or a villa in some remote Spanish resort. While this could turn out to be everything they hoped for, and more, many people rush full steam ahead without any real assessment of the pros and cons.

Before you come to any definite decision, first ask yourself a few down-to-earth questions. What are your main priorities? To be closer to your family? To have a smaller, more manageable home that will be easier to run – and less expensive? To realise some capital in order to provide you with extra money for your retirement? To live in a specific town or village, which you know you like and where you have plenty of friends?

Or to enjoy the security of being in accommodation that offers some of the facilities you may want as you become older, such as a resident caretaker and the option of having some of your meals catered?

Staying put

While there may be plenty of arguments for moving, there are probably just as many for staying where you are. Moving home can be a traumatic experience at the best of times and even more so as you become older, when precious possessions are more painful to part with, as is usually the necessity when moving somewhere smaller.

Although ideally you may want to remain where you are, you may feel that your home is too large or inconvenient for you to manage in the future. Before rushing to put it on the market, it is worth considering whether there are ways of adapting it to provide what you want. You might think about re-using the space in a better way. Would it be possible, for example, to convert a spare room into a work den and get rid of the clutter from the main living area? Have you thought about letting one or two rooms? As well as solving the problem of wasted space, it would also bring in some extra income.

A few improvements invested in now could make all the difference in terms of comfort and practicality. Many of us make do with inefficient heating systems that could be improved relatively easily and cheaply. Stairs need not necessarily be a problem, even when you are very much older, thanks to modern stair lifts. Even so, a few basic facilities installed on the ground floor could save your legs in years to come. Similarly, gardens can be replanned: extending the lawn or paving could spare you hours of exhausting weeding.

Moving to a new home

If you do decide to move, the sooner you start looking the better. With time to spare, you will have a greater choice of properties and more chance to weigh up the pros and cons.

While a smaller house will almost certainly be easier and cheaper to run, make sure it is not so small that you will feel cramped. When you are both at home, you may need more room to avoid getting on top of each other.

Also if your family lives some distance away, you may want the space to have them to stay.

If you are thinking of moving to a new neighbourhood, points to consider are: access to shops, proximity to friends, availability of public transport and whether the area offers the leisure facilities you enjoy.

Counting the cost

Moving house is expensive. It is estimated that the cost is between 5 and 10 per cent of the value of a new home, once you have totted up such extras as removal charges, insurance, stamp duty, VAT, legal fees and estate agents' commission. If you plan any repairs or decorations, the figure will be considerably higher.

A good tip to remember is that stamp duty (which applies to all properties costing more than £60,000) is not levied on fitments such as carpets and curtains. If you are considering a purchase which includes some of these, try to negotiate a separate price for them.

When buying a new home, it is essential to have a full building (structural) survey. This will cost around £400 for a small terraced house but is worth every penny. In particular, it will give you protection in law should things go wrong.

Bridging loans

Tempting as it may be to buy before you sell, unless you have the money to finance the cost of two homes – including possibly two mortgages – you need to do your sums very carefully indeed.

Banks usually charge 3 points or more over base rate plus an arrangement or administration fee on top. So, if bank rate is 7 per cent, the interest charged on a £100,000 loan works out at £833 a month; or £5,000 if it takes you six months to sell.

As an alternative to bridging loans, some estate agents may offer to buy your home at a discount. You would be 'selling on the cheap' and, while this could make sense, it is not a decision to be taken lightly.

Removal firms

Costs can vary considerably, so it pays to shop around and get at least three quotes. It is important to check exactly what you are paying for and whether the price includes packing and insurance.

A list of approved firms can be obtained from: **British Association of Removers**, 3 Churchill Court, 58 Station Road, North Harrow HA2 7SA. T:0181 861 3331 (please enclose sae).

Moving in with family or friends

There are many advantages to such an arrangement. While you are active, you can contribute to the household. Should you become frail or ill, help will be at hand.

Problems can also arise, however. As a precaution, try to work out in advance any potential conflicts. Questions to consider include: whether you will eat together; whether you will contribute in practical ways, like baby-sitting or shopping; also, whether you can keep a pet and have friends to stay.

Money is also a common source of dispute. Decide whether you will have your own telephone – or share one. If you will be paying rent, make it a formal arrangement exactly as if you were a normal tenant. You must agree a set figure: what it will cover, how it will be assessed in future and how it will be paid, i.e. weekly, monthly, cash or standing order. It is advisable to check with a solicitor or housing advice centre how sharing might affect your rights and obligations as either landlord or tenant. In particular, you should take advice before embarking on any construction work which might affect the property's exemption from capital gains tax in the future.

Retirement housing and sheltered accommodation

The term 'retirement' or 'sheltered accommodation' generally means property with a resident warden/caretaker, an emergency alarm system, optional meals and some communal facilities such as living rooms, garden and laundry. Guest accommodation and services such as hairdressers and chiropodists are sometimes also available.

Much of the property is run by local authorities, housing associations and charities. There are also many private developments, for sale or rent, at prices to suit most pockets. Some useful addresses are given in Chapter 11.

Making your home more practical

It is sensible to set about any home improvement plans earlier rather than later. For one thing, these are often easier to afford when you are still earning a regular salary. For another, any building work is tiresome and most people find it easier to put up with the mess when they are not living among it 24 hours a day. Thirdly, if you start early, you will enjoy the benefit that much sooner.

Insulation

Heat escapes from a building in four main ways: through the roof, walls, floor and through loose-fitting doors and windows. Insulation will not only cut the heat loss but will usually more than pay for itself within four or five years.

Loft insulation Insulating materials are readily available from builders merchants. Or to employ a specialist, contact the **National**

Association of Loft Insulation Contractors, PO Box 12, Haslemere, Surrey GU27 3AH. T:01428 654011.

Doors and windows. The two most effective ways of saving heat loss are double-glazing and draught-proofing. You could buy DIY products. Or if using a contractor, contact: **Glass and Glazing Federation**, 44-48 Borough High Street, London SE1 1XB. T:0171 403 7177; **Draught Proofing Advisory Association**, PO Box 12, Haslemere, Surrey GU27·3AH. T:01428 654011.

Walls. More heat is lost through the walls than perhaps anywhere else in the house. Wall insulation (whether cavity or solid walls) is work for a specialist and, though expensive, should cut your heating bill by about a quarter.

For further information and addresses of registered contractors, contact:

External Wall Insulation Association, PO Box 12, Haslemere, Surrey GU27 3AH. T:01428 654011 – for solid or defective walls.

Cavity Foam Bureau, PO Box 79, Oldbury, Warley, West Midlands B69 4PW. T:0121 544 4949.

Floor insulation. Up to 15 per cent of heat loss can be saved by filling cracks in the floorboards and skirting. Be careful not to block up the underfloor ventilation which protects floor timbers from dampness and rot.

Hot water cylinder insulation. You can save several pounds a week by insulating your hot water cylinder. Jacket should be at least 80mm thick and carry the BSI kitemark and BS 5615.

Heating

Your local gas and electricity showrooms, and also Solid Fuel Advisory Council office, can advise on most matters to do with heating and hot water systems.

Buying and installing heating equipment. Faulty heating systems and slip-shod installations can kill. When buying equipment, check that it has been approved by the appropriate standards board.

For electrical equipment, the letters to look for are BEAB or CCA. For gas appliances, either buy from a British Gas Energy Centres shop or, if buying elsewhere, look for the BSI kitemark. Domestic solid fuel equipment should be approved by the Solid Fuel Appliances Approval Scheme (see sales literature).

It is also essential to check that the contractor who installs your equipment is registered. The following organisations should be able to help with local names and addresses:

National Inspection Council for Electrical Installation Contracting, Vintage House, 37 Albert Embankment, London SE1 7UJ. T:0171 582 7746.

Electrical Contractors Association, 34 Palace Court, London W2 4HY. T:0171 229 1266.

Council for Registered Gas Installers, 1 Elm Wood, Chineham Business Park, Crockford Lane, Basingstoke, Hants RG24 8WG. T:01256 372200.

Solid Fuel Advisory Service and (for oil central heating) the **Approved Coal Merchants Scheme** (see local telephone directory).

Heating and Ventilating Contractors' Association, (for all types of central heating), ESCA House, 34 Palace Court, London W2 4JG. T:0171 229 2488; or call the **Home Heating Linkline** (all calls charged at local rate) on 0345 581158.

Useful reading
Helping Your Environment. Two booklets with advice on insulation and heating systems; available free from PO Box 200, Stratford-upon-Avon, Warwickshire CV37 9ZZ.

Tips for reducing your energy bills

Energy can be saved in lots of small ways. Taken together, they could amount to quite a large cut in your heating bills. You may find some of the following ideas worth considering:

■ Set your central heating timer and thermostat to suit the weather. A saving of half an hour or one degree can be substantial.

■ A separate thermostat on your hot water cylinder set at around 60 degrees Centigrade will enable you to keep hot water for taps at a lower temperature than for the heating system.

■ If you run your hot water off an immersion heater, have a timeswitch fitted attached to an Economy 7 meter so that the water is heated at the cheap rate overnight. An override switch will enable you to top up the heat during the day if necessary.

■ Showers are more economical than baths as well as being easier to use when you become older.

■ Reflective foil sheets put behind your radiators help to reduce heat loss through the walls.

- Switch off or reduce the heating in rooms not being used.
- An electric casserole is economical for single households. Pressure cookers and microwave ovens can save fuel and time.
- Finally, it is a good idea to get in the habit of reading your electricity and gas meters regularly. This will help you keep track of likely bills.

Improvement and repair

Building work is notoriously expensive. It is worth investigating whether you could take advantage of some of the available grants.

Improvement and repair grants

Excepting certain items applicable to Disabled Facilities Grant, all grants are discretionary.

Renovation grant. There are seven main eventualities where application for a grant might be successful: (1) to bring a property up to a standard of fitness for human habitation; (2) for works to comply with a statutory repairs notice served on the owner; (3) to replace or repair rotten or defective parts of the structure including, for example, doors, windows, walls, an ineffective damp-proof course or unsatisfactory wiring; (4) for home insulation; (5) to provide heating facilities; (6) for the provision of satisfactory internal arrangements such as improvement of a very steep or winding staircase; (7) for conversions, such as the creation of a self-contained flat.

All claims for grant are at the discretion of the council. Eligibility is means-tested and different tests apply according to whether the applicant is an owner-occupier or tenant or whether he/she is a landlord. An individual's resources are taken into account in determining the actual amount of grant, which could only make a tiny contribution to the cost of the works – or might pay for everything.

The property must have been built or converted at least ten years before the date of application for grant. Second homes do not qualify.

Common parts grant. This is for the improvement or repair of the common parts of a building containing one or more flats. Items that normally count as 'common parts' include the roof, lift, staircase and entrance lobby. Grant can be applied for either by a landlord and/or by at least three-quarters of the occupying tenants. Tenants' financial resources are taken into account and (where applicable) the property must have been converted at least ten years previously.

HMO grant. This can only be applied for by a landlord and is for the improvement of Houses in Multiple Occupation; or for the conversion of a property for HMO use.

Disabled facilities grant. This is designed to adapt or provide facilities for a home (including the common parts) to make it more suitable for occupation by a disabled person. Grant can cover a wide range, including: work to facilitate access; the provision of suitable bathroom or kitchen facilities; the adaptation of heating or lighting controls; improvement of the heating system.

Provided the applicant is eligible, a mandatory grant of up to £20,000 may be available for all the above (councils may use their discretion to award more). Discretionary grant is also available for a variety of other works where these would make a home suitable for a disabled person.

The individual must be registered (or registrable) as disabled. There is a means test. The council will want to check that the proposed work is reasonable and practicable for the age/condition of the property and the social services department will need to be satisfied that the works are necessary and appropriate to meet the individual's needs.

Eligibility for all the above grants depends on the validity of the proposed work and on the applicant's resources, taking into account their income and any savings over £5,000.

How to apply. Contact the Home Improvement Section of your local council for an application form.

Before making an application, you should read the D of E booklet on renovation grants (available from the council) which explains the requirements in detail and also suggests sources such as your Citizens' Advice Bureau that can help you assess your likelihood of qualifying and advise you of any preliminary steps (such as getting estimates) you need to take. Even if they are highly optimistic of your chances of obtaining a grant, **do not start work until approval has been given.**

Home repair assistance. This is a new grant which has replaced Minor Works Assistance grant. It can help pay for small but essential works to your home, including: (1) to provide or improve thermal insulation; (2) to repair, improve or adapt a property to enable people over 60 to remain in their own home; (3) as 2, if you have an older, or disabled, person coming to live with you permanently.

A grant is normally only available to owner-occupiers and private sector tenants who are in receipt of income support or similar benefit. People with a right to live in the dwelling for more than five years may be eligible if they lived there for three years prior to making the application.

Maximum grant is £2,000 per application, up to a total of £4,000 over three years. For further information and application form, contact your Housing Department. **N.B.** Do not start on any improvement until your council has informed you that your application has been approved.

Community care grant. Income support recipients may be able to obtain a community care grant from the Social Fund to help with repairs. For further information, see leaflet SFL2 *How the Social Fund Can Help You*, obtainable from your local Benefits Agency office.

Grants for the sick and disabled

Your local authority may be able to help with the provision of certain special facilities such as a stair lift, telephone installations or a ramp to replace steps. Apply to your Social Services Department.

Useful addresses

The Building Centre, 26 Store Street, London WC1E 7BT. T:0171 637 1022. Displays wide range of building products and appliances, has manufacturers' lists and can also advise about building problems.

Federation of Master Builders (FMB), Gordon Fisher House, 14-15 Great James Street, London WC1N 3DP. T:0171 242 7583. Lists of members are available from regional offices.

Guild of Master Craftsmen, Castle Place, 166 High Street, Lewes, East Sussex BN7 1XU. T:01273 478449. Can supply names of all types of specialist craftsmen.

Institute of Plumbing, 64 Station Lane, Hornchurch, Essex RM12 6NB. T:01708 472791. Can provide a list of registered plumbers; sae appreciated.

The Scottish and Northern Ireland Plumbing Employers' Federation, 2 Walker Street, Edinburgh EH3 7LB. T:0131 225 2255. Includes almost 1,000 plumbing and domestic heating firms. Lists of local members supplied on request.

Royal Institution of Chartered Surveyors, The RICS Information Centre, Surveyor Court, Westwood Way, Coventry CV4 8JE. T:0171 222 7000. Can nominate qualified local surveyors. Also publishes a number of useful leaflets.

Royal Institute of British Architects, 66 Portland Place, London W1N 4AD. T:0171 580 5533. Has a free Clients' Advisory Service and can recommend suitable architects.

The British Wood Preserving and Damp-Proofing Association (BWPDA), Building No. 6, The Office Village, 4 Romford Road, Stratford, London E15 4EA. T:0181 519 2588. Can advise on anything to do with wood preservation and damp-proofing in the home.

Home Improvement Agencies

Home Improvement Agencies (sometimes known as 'Care and Repair' or 'Staying Put' projects) exist in many areas to help older or disabled house owners repair and adapt their homes. They will help to assess your needs, get a builder, supervise the work, raise the finance and check the completed job. For advice about local schemes, contact: Care and Repair, Castle House, Kirtley Drive, Nottingham NG7 1LD. T:0115 979 9091; Care and Repair Cymru, Norbury House, Fairwater, Cardiff CF5 3AS. T:01222 576286; Anchor Trust, Fountain Court, Oxford Spires Business Park, Kidlington, Oxon OX5 1NZ. T:01865 854000.

Safety in the home

Accidents in the home account for 40 per cent of all fatal accidents. The vast majority are caused by carelessness or by danger spots in the home that for the most part could very easily be made safer.

Steps and stairs should be well lit and have a handrail along the wall to provide extra support. Frayed carpet on staircases should be repaired or replaced soonest.

Floors: rugs and mats can slip on polished floors and should always be laid on some form of non-slip backing material. Spilt water or talcum powder on tiled or linoleum floors is a number one cause of accidents.

The **bathroom** is another danger zone. Sensible precautionary measures include using a suction-type bath mat and putting handrails on the bath or alongside the shower. A bath seat can be helpful for older people. Soap on a rope is safer in a shower.

Fires can all too easily start in the home. If you have an open fire, you should always use a fireguard and sparkguard at night; and chimneys should be swept at least once a year. Upholstered furniture is a particular hazard. If buying new, make sure that it carries a red triangle label.

Portable heaters should be kept away from furniture and curtains and placed where you cannot trip over them. Paraffin heaters should be never be filled while alight. Avoid leaving paraffin where it will be exposed to heat; if possible, keep it in a metal container outside the house.

Gas appliances should be regularly serviced. Ensure there is adequate ventilation when using heaters. Never block up air vents: carbon monoxide fumes can kill.

A free safety check on gas appliances is available to anyone living alone who is over the age of 60 or registered disabled; or living with other people where everyone, like themselves, is either over 60 or registered disabled. To arrange a check contact your local British Gas Home Energy office (see your last gas bill for telephone number).

More than one in three fires in the home are due to accidents with cookers. Pan handles should be turned away from the heat and positioned so you cannot knock them off the stove. If called to the door or telephone, always take the pan off the ring and turn off the heat.

Cigarettes left smouldering in a full ashtray could be dangerous. Smoking in bed is a potential killer!

Faulty **electric wiring** is another frequent cause of fires, as are overloaded power points. Wiring needs checking every five years and avoid using too many appliances off a single plug. (Ask an electrician's advice.) Plugs should conform to British Standard 1365 and frayed or damaged flexes immediately replaced.

As a general precaution, keep **fire extinguishers** handy and make sure they are maintained in working order. They should conform to the British Standard 5423 or BS 5306 part 3. Many insurance companies now recommend that you install a smoke alarm as an effective and cheap early warning device. Prices start from about £5.

Home security

The Crime Prevention Officer at your local police station will be glad to advise you how to improve your security arrangements.

The most vulnerable access points are doors and windows. Doors should have secure bolts or a five lever deadlock, strengthened by metal plates on both sides, a door chain and a spyhole. You might also consider outside lights to illuminate night-time visitors and an entryphone so you can check who is at the door.

Windows should ideally have key-operated locks that secure them when partially open; french windows need rack bolts or surface-mounted security pressbolts. You could also have window-bars and shutters.

Ensure the house is securely locked whenever you go out. Insist that official callers such as meter men show their identity cards before you allow them inside. If you are going away remember to cancel the milk and the newspapers. You might also consider using the Royal Mail's **Keepsafe** service for letters; ask at the post office.

For names of reputable locksmiths, contact: **Master Locksmiths Association**, Units 4-5, The Business Park, Woodford Halse, Daventry, Northants NN11 3PZ. T:01327 262255.

Burglar alarms and safes

Many insurance companies will recommend suitable contractors to install burglar alarm equipment. Alternatively, contact: **The National Approval Council for Security Systems (NACOSS)**, Queensgate House, 14 Cookham Road, Maidenhead, Berks SL6 8AJ, T:01628 37512.

If you keep valuables or money in the house, you should think about buying a concealed wall or floor safe.

Insurance

Seven out of ten householders are under-insured, some of them unknowingly but some intentionally to keep premiums lower. While understandable when money is tight, this has to be foolhardy. A better solution by far is to see whether you could obtain better terms than you are getting at present.

Some insurance companies offer Retired Householders Insurance Policies at substantially reduced rates. These are arranged through **Age Concern Insurance Services**, Garrod House, Chaldon Road, Caterham CR3 5YZ; and through **Hill House Hammond Ltd.**, Retired Householders Insurance Department, Freepost, Lewins Mead, Bristol BS1 2BR. **Saga Services Ltd.**, The Saga Building, Middelburg Square, Folkestone, Kent CT20 1AZ, T:0800 414 525, promises customers over 50 that it will refund the difference if they can find a cheaper policy, offering the same cover, within two months of taking Saga insurance.

Many insurers also give discounts for installation of proper security precautions; some award extra points if the householder joins a Neighbourhood Watch Scheme. For names of brokers write to: **Institute of Insurance Brokers**, Higham Business Centre, Midland Road, Higham Ferrers, Northants NN10 8DW. T:01933 410003.

There are also appreciable savings with excess policies, i.e. where the householder pays the first chunk of any claim, say, the first £100 or £250.

Some people pay more than they need because they forget to cancel items which they have given away or sold. Equally, many forget to add new valuables they have bought or received as presents. You should also check that you are adequately covered for any home improvements you may have added.

An even more vital point is to ensure that your policy has not lapsed. If the insurance was originally arranged through your building society it may cease when your mortgage is paid off, in which case it will be essential for you to arrange new cover direct. Similarly, when buying for cash – for instance when moving to a smaller house – it will be up to you to organise the insurance and to calculate the rebuilding value of your home. It is advisable to get a qualified valuer to do this for you.

The **Association of British Insurers**, 51 Gresham Street, London EC2V 7HQ. T:0171 600 3333 will send you free information sheets on household insurance which describe what policies you need and indicate the correct amount of cover. Enclose sae.

The **British Insurance and Investment Brokers Association**, BIIBA House, 14 Bevis Marks, London EC3A 7NT. T:0171 623 9043, can send you a list of insurance brokers in your area.

Letting rooms in your home

Many people whose home has become too large are tempted by the idea of taking in tenants. For some, it is an ideal plan; for others, a disaster. At best, it could provide you with extra income and the possibility of pleasant company. At worst, you could be involved in a lengthy legal battle to regain possession of your property.

There are three broad choices: taking in paying guests or lodgers; letting part of your home as self-contained accommodation; or renting the whole house for a set period of time. In all cases for your own protection it is essential to have a written agreement and to take up bank references, unless the let is a strictly temporary one where the money is paid in advance. Otherwise, rent should be collected quarterly and you should arrange a hefty deposit to cover any damage.

To encourage more people to let out rooms in their home, the Government now allows you to earn up to £4,250 a year free of tax. For further information, see Inland Revenue booklet IR 87 *Rooms To Let*, available from any tax office.

Finally, if you have a mortgage or are a tenant yourself (even with a very long lease), confirm with your building society or landlord that you are entitled to sublet.

Paying guests or lodgers. This is the most informal arrangement with few legal formalities involved. Also as a resident owner, you are in a very strong position if you want your lodger to leave.

You would be wise to check with your insurance company about your home contents policy, as some insurers restrict cover to households with lodgers. Also, inform your lodger that his/her possessions are not covered by your policy.

Holiday lets. It is a good idea to register with your Tourist Information Centre and to contact the Environmental Health Office at your local council for any help and advice.

Useful reading
Want to Rent A Room? DoE leaflet, available from libraries, housing advice centres and Citizens' Advice Bureaux.

Letting part of your home. You could convert a basement or part of your house as a self-contained flat and let this either furnished or unfurnished.

As long as you or a member of your family continue to live in the house you will be in much the same position as if you had a paying guest. As a resident landlord, you have a guaranteed right to repossession of your property. If the letting was for a fixed term (e.g. six months or a year), the tenancy will automatically cease at the end of the fixed period. If the arrangement was more casual, it may be advisable to give at least four weeks' notice in writing. For further information, see DoE housing booklets No.24 *Notice That You Must Leave* and No. 22 *Letting Rooms in Your Home,* available from CABs.

Tax note. If you later sell your home, you may not be able to claim exemption from capital gains tax on the increase in value of a flat if it is entirely self-contained. A solution is to retain some means of access to the main house or flat, but take legal advice as to what will qualify.

Renting out your home on a temporary basis. If you are thinking of spending the winter in the sun or are considering buying a retirement home for the future, you might be tempted by the idea of letting the whole house. To avoid many of the problems, you should write the lease under the new assured shorthold tenancy rules; see housing booklet *Assured Tenancies: a Guide for Landlords*. It is strongly advisable to ask a solicitor to help you draw up the agreement. A useful leaflet is *Letting Your Home is Now Easier and Safer*, available from your local housing department.

Holiday lets

Buying a future retirement home in the country and renting it out as a holiday home is another option worth considering. As well as providing you with a weekend cottage at other times of the year, it can also prove a useful and profitable investment.

There are various attractive tax advantages which an accountant would explain. An important condition is that the property must be available for letting for at least 140 days during the tax year and be actually let for at least 70 days.

Housing benefit

Provided you have no more than £16,000 in savings, you may be able to get help with your rent from your local council. You may qualify for housing benefit whether you are a council or private tenant or live in a hotel or hostel. The amount you get depends on: your income; your capital or savings; the number of people in your household; your eligible rent; and your 'applicable amount', which is the amount of money the government considers you need for basic living expenses. At its most generous, benefit could be for the whole amount of your eligible rent.

Applicable amount. Your 'applicable amount' will generally be the same as the amount of income support for which you would be eligible. For details, see leaflet NI 196, obtainable from your Social Security office.

How to claim. If you think you might be eligible for benefit, ask your council for an application form. Among other information, you will need to give particulars of the property where you hope to stay – or plan to move. The council should let you know within 14 days of receiving your completed application whether you are entitled to benefit and, if so, will inform you of the amount.

If you make a claim for income support you can claim housing benefit and council tax benefit at the same time. A claim form for these is included inside the income support claim form.

If you need any help or advice in understanding the forms, ask at your CAB or local Age Concern group.

Useful reading
Leaflet RR 2 *A Guide to Housing Benefit and Council Tax Benefit,* free from any Social Security office.

Council tax

Council tax is based on the value of the dwelling in which you live (the property element) and also a personal element – with discounts/exemptions applying to certain groups of people.

The property element. The value of the property is assessed according to a banding system, with eight different bands (A to H).

The valuation of each property is administered by the Inland Revenue Valuation Office. The ascribed value is based on prices applying at 1 April 1991. Small extensions/other improvements made after this date do not affect the valuation. New homes are banded as if they had already been built and sold on 1 April 1991. If you think there has been a misunderstanding about the valuation (or your liability to pay the full amount) you have the right of appeal. See 'appeals' further along.

The personal element. Not everyone pays council tax. The bill is normally sent to the owner, or joint owners, of the property; or in the case of rented accommodation, to the tenant or joint tenants; or in the case of licensed property, to the residents or joint residents.

In some cases, for example in hostels or multi occupied property, a landlord or owner may pass on a share of the bill to the tenants/residents which would probably be included as part of the rental charge.

The valuation of each dwelling assumes two adults are resident. The charge does not increase if there are more adults. However if, as in many homes, there is just one adult, your council tax bill will be reduced by 25 per cent.

There are also a number of other special discounts, or exemptions, as follows:

- People who are severely mentally impaired qualify for a 25 per cent discount;
- Disabled people who require additional space may have their bill reduced to a lower band;
- People on income support should normally have nothing to pay, as their bill will be met in full by the benefit;
- Disabled people on higher rate attendance allowance need not count a full-time carer as an additional resident and therefore may continue to qualify for the 25 per cent single (adult) householder discount; exceptions are spouses/partners and parents of a disabled child under 18 who would normally be living with the disabled person and whose presence therefore would not be adding to the council tax;
- Young people over 18 but still at school are not counted when assessing the number of adults in a house;
- Students living in halls of residence, student hostels or similar are exempted; those living with a parent or other non-student adult are eligible for the 25 per cent personal discount;
- Service personnel living in barracks or married quarters will not receive any bill for council tax.

Discounts/exemptions applying to property

Certain property is either exempt from council tax or is eligible for a discount.

Discounts. Empty property (e.g. second homes) normally gets a 50 per cent discount. There are some exceptions where empty property is treated more generously – see exemptions below.

Exemptions. The most common cases of exemptions include:

- Property in course of being built or undergoing major structural alteration/repair: the exemption will last until 6 months after the work is completed;
- Property which has been unoccupied and unfurnished for less than six months;
- Home of a deceased person: the exemption lasts until 6 months after the grant of probate;
- Home that is empty because the occupier is absent in order to care for someone else;
- Home of a person who is/would be exempted from council tax due to moving to a residential home or similar;
- Granny flats that are part of another private domestic dwelling may be exempt but this depends on access and other conditions. To check, contact your local Valuation Office.

Business-cum-domestic property

Business-cum-domestic property is rated according to usage, with the business section assessed for business rates and the domestic section for council tax. For example, where there is a flat over a shop, the value of the shop would not be included in the valuation for council tax.

Appeals

People who feel they have been wrongly assessed for council tax on one of the following four grounds have the right of appeal: (1) if you become the new person responsible for paying the tax on a property (e.g. because you have moved) that you think has been wrongly banded; (2) if there has been a material increase or reduction in the property's value; (3) if you start, or stop, using the property for business; (4) if either of the latter two apply and the listing officer has altered the council tax without giving you a chance to put your side.

You should take up the matter with the valuation office (see local telephone directory). If you are still unhappy, you can then appeal to an independent valuation tribunal. For advice and further information, contact your CAB.

For further information, see leaflets: *Council Tax: A Guide to Your Bill* and *Council Tax: A Guide to Valuation, Banding and Appeals,* obtainable free from any council office.

Council tax benefit

If you cannot afford your council tax because you have a low income, you may be able to obtain council tax benefit. The help is more generous than many people realise. For example, people on income support are entitled to rebates of up to 100 per cent. The amount you would get depends on: your income, savings, your personal circumstances, who else lives in your home (in particular whether they would be counted as a 'non-dependant') and on your net council tax bill. If you are not sure whether your income is low enough to qualify, it is worth claiming as you could be pleasantly surprised. If you disagree with your council's decision, you can ask for this to be reviewed. If you still think your council has made a mistake, you can ask for a further review by a local Review Board.

For further information, ask your local Social Security office for leaflet CTB 1 *Help with the Council Tax*.

Useful organisations

The following should be able to provide general advice about housing and help with housing problems:

- Local Authority Housing Departments
- Housing Advice or Housing Aid Centres
- Citizens' Advice Bureaux
- Local Authority Social Service Departments if your problem is linked to disability
- Welfare Rights Centres if your problem, for example, concerns a landlord who does not keep the property properly maintained
- Local councillors and MPs.

8

Leisure Activities to Enjoy

Whether you are looking forward to devoting more time to an existing interest, resuming an old hobby or trying your hand at something new, the choice is enormous.

The ideas in this chapter are just a small sample. Your library, local authority recreation department and adult education institute will be able to signpost you to other activities in your area.

While every effort has been made to ensure that prices are correct, those quoted should only be taken as a guide. The reason is that most organisations alter their charges from time to time and since there is no set date, it is impossible to keep track.

Adult education

Ever longed to take a degree, learn about computing, study art or do a language course? Opportunities abound with these and scores of other subjects available to everyone, regardless of age.

Adult Education Institutes

There is an Adult Education Institute in most areas. Classes normally start in September and run through the academic year. Many AEIs allow concessionary fees for students over 60. Ask your library for details. Or in London, buy *Floodlight* (£3.50), available from most bookstalls.

National Adult School Organisation, Masu Centre, Gaywood Croft, Cregoe Street, Birmingham B15 2ED. T:0121 622 3400. Their 'Friendship Through Discussion' groups meet in members' homes or in halls, weekly or fortnightly. Some groups organise social activities and there is also a national summer school. For further information, write to the above address, enclosing sae.

National Extension College, 18 Brooklands Avenue, Cambridge CB2 2HN. T:01223 316644. A choice of over 150 home study courses are listed in the NEC's free Guide, available on request. Cost is £75 upwards, with a discount for pensioners on the more expensive.

Open University, Course Reservations and Sales Centre, PO Box 200, Walton Hall, Milton Keynes MK7 6YZ. T:01908 653231. Students are all ages – the oldest OU graduate was 92 – no academic qualifications are required and there is a vast range of subjects from which to choose.

Courses normally involve a mix of: correspondence work, radio and TV programmes, audio and video cassettes, contact with local tutors and, in some cases, also a residential school.

University of the Third Age, U3A National Office, 26 Harrison Street, London WC1H 8JG. T:0171 837 8838. U3A offers a wide range of educational, creative and leisure activities. It operates through a national network of local U3As, which choose their own courses and social programmes according to members' interests. Individuals may join as Associates for £5 per annum. For a brochure, contact the address above enclosing a 6″ x 10″ sae.

Workers' Educational Association, Temple House, 17 Victoria Park Square, Bethnal Green, London E2 9PB. T:0181 983 1515. Offers a wide range of day and evening courses. Your library or education authority should be able to put you in touch with your local branch.

Arts

You can enjoy a glorious choice of events with many offering concessionary prices to retired people.

Regional arts boards and local arts councils

For first hand information about what is going on in your area, contact your regional arts board; or in the case of those living in Scotland, Wales and Northern Ireland, the national arts council. Most areas arrange an immensely varied programme with musical events, drama, arts and craft exhibitions and sometimes more unusual functions, offering something of interest to just about everyone. Many regional arts boards produce regular newsletters with details of events in their area. For addresses, ask at your local library

Music and ballet

Scope ranges from becoming a Friend and supporting one of the famous 'Houses' such as Covent Garden to music-making in your own right.

Friends enjoy some very attractive advantages including in all cases priority for bookings.

Friends of Covent Garden, Royal Opera House, Covent Garden, London WC2E 9DD. T:0171 212 9412. Friends may attend talks, recitals, study days and certain 'open' rehearsals. Reduced price tickets (short notice). Annual membership is £45. From September 1997 to late 1999 The Royal Ballet and The Royal Opera will be performing at a number of other London venues while the Royal Opera House is closed for redevelopment.

Friends of English National Opera, London Coliseum, St. Martin's Lane, London WC2N 4ES. T:0171 632 8300. Friends enjoy a variety of special lunch-time and evening events. Membership (standard) costs £25 a year.

Friends of Sadler's Wells, Lion House, 23 Islington High Street, London N1 9LG. T:0171 278 1152. Friends are invited to open rehearsals, talks and social functions and also enjoy ticket concessions. Annual membership at pension age costs £12.

Music making

Just about every kind of musical taste can be met. Information about local societies and other groups is contained in the *British Music Education Year Book* and the *British Music Year Book*, both of which should be in the reference section of your library.

Handbell Ringers of Great Britain, 87 The Woodfields, Sanderstead, South Croydon, Surrey CR2 0HJ. T:0181 651 2663. Arranges concerts, rallies, seminars and workshops. To contact your local group, write to the above address, enclosing sae.

National Federation of Music Societies, Francis House, Francis Street, London SW1P 1DE. T:0171 828 7320. Can provide you with addresses of some 1,700 choral societies, orchestras and music societies throughout the country. Most charge a nominal membership fee and standards range from the semi-professional to the unashamedly amateur.

Society of Recorder Players, 15 Palliser Road, London W14 9EB. T:0171 385 7321. Players of all standards and ages are welcomed at the many branches. For list of addresses, please enclose sae. Annual subscription is £10. Branch membership varies.

Television and radio audiences

If you would like to be part of an invited studio audience, apply to the BBC through the relevant ticket unit for London-based programmes; or for outside London, through the appropriate regional centre. The ticket unit addresses are:

The Ticket Unit, **BBC Television Audience Services**, Wood Lane, Shepherd's Bush, London W12 7RJ.

The Ticket Unit, **BBC Radio**, Broadcasting House, London W1A 1AA.

For independent television, audience participation is the responsibility of each programme maker and requests should be channelled to the contractor for the area.

Theatre

Theatre tickets need not cost a fortune! Preview performances are invariably cheaper and there are often concessionary rates for matinees. Herewith just a couple of places that offer special facilities of interest.

Barbican Centre, Silk Street, London EC2Y 8DS. T:0171 638 4141 (for information). Box office: 0171 638 8891. The Centre has two theatres, concert hall, art gallery, cinemas and library. There are often free live musical events and exhibitions. Pensioners can buy reduced tickets on a standby basis. Mailing list subscribers pay £7 a year.

Royal National Theatre, South Bank, London SE1 9PX. T:0171 928 2252 (box office). Offers a host of attractive facilities as well as its three theatres. There are group price reductions for most performances and pensioners can buy matinee seats from £10. For membership details, contact Royal National Theatre, Mailing List, Freepost, London SE1 7BR.

Society of London Theatre, Bedford Chambers, The Piazza, Covent Garden, London WC2E 8HQ. T:0171 836 0971. The Society co-ordinates a scheme under which senior citizens can get substantial reductions for midweek matinee performances at many West End theatres and also concessionary prices for other performances on a standby basis. Look for symbols 'M' and 'S' in the *London Theatre Guide* (annual subscription £12.50, from the Society).

Concessions are subject to availability, so best check with the box office first. Senior citizens will need to show a travel pass or pension book as proof of their age.

The Society's *Disabled Access Guide to London West End Theatres* provides information about special facilities, access for wheelchairs and transport advice for disabled theatregoers. Available free from SOLT (please send 49p sae).

Leicester Square Ticket Booth, London. Sells tickets to many West End theatres at half-price on the day of performance. It is open to personal callers, Monday to Saturday at 12 noon – 6.30 p.m.; or in the case of matinees, until 1/2 hour before starting time. There is a service charge of £2. Payment in cash only.

Late night trains. Late night trains for theatregoers run from many London stations. For details of services, enquire at your local station.

Visual arts

If you enjoy attending exhibitions and lectures, membership of some of the arts societies offers you a number of delightful privileges.

Contemporary Art Society, 17 Bloomsbury Square, London WC1A 2LP. T:0171 831 7311. Members can take part in an extensive programme of events including visits to artists' studios and parties at special exhibitions. Annual subscription is £30, £35 per couple.

National Art Collections Fund, Millais House, 7 Cromwell Place, London SW7 2JN. T:0171 225 4800. Members enjoy free admission to many museums and galleries plus a countrywide programme of lectures, private views and other special events. There are also art tours at home and abroad led by experts. Subscription is £25 a year; senior citizens, £18.

National Association of Decorative & Fine Arts Societies, NADFAS House, 8 Guilford Street, London WC1N 1DT. T:0171 430 0730. Events include lectures, museum and gallery visits, guided tours of historic houses and organised tours in the UK and abroad. Membership of a local society is about £20-£28 a year. Details are available from NADFAS, see above.

Royal Academy of Arts, Piccadilly, London W1V 0DS. T:0171 439 7438. Senior citizens enjoy reduced entrance charges to all exhibitions. Alternatively, you could buy an 'Academy Card' (£17) which allows free entrance to any five exhibitions over 18 months; or become a Friend (£40 for people over 60) with invitations to private views plus tours, lectures and use of the Friend's Room for coffee.

Crafts

As well as being fun, proficiency in a craft is a means of beautifying your home – or can even develop into a flourishing cottage industry.

The Basketmakers' Association, Hon. Secretary: Mrs Ann Brooks, Pond Cottage, North Road, Chesham Bois, Amersham, Bucks HP6 5NA. T:01494 726189. Promotes the art of basket-making, chair seating and allied crafts. It arranges courses, demonstrations and exhibitions. Membership costs £10.

Crafts Council, 44A Pentonville Road, Islington, London N1 9BY. T:0171 278 7700. The Crafts Council runs an information centre and reference library which can give advice on just about everything you could want to know: courses, suppliers of materials, addresses of craft guilds and societies, fact sheets on business practice as well as details of craft fairs and markets, galleries, shops and other outlets for work.

The Embroiderers' Guild, Apartment 41, Hampton Court Palace, East Molesey, Surrey KT8 9AU. T:0181 943 1229. Members can visit the collection of embroideries at Hampton Court, borrow study folios and attend classes and lectures. There is also a full programme of residential weekends, seminars and tours; plus 160 local branches. Membership for those over 60 is £17.50.

West Dean College, West Dean, Chichester, West Sussex PO18 0QZ. T:01243 811301. Organises short residential courses in art, craft and music. A typical programme includes: stained glass, calligraphy, textile design, woodcarving, blacksmithing, jewellery and many more. Prices, which include full board, start from about £150.

Dance/keep fit

Clubs, classes and groups exist in all parts of the country, variously offering: ballroom, Old Tyme, Scottish, folk, ballet, disco dancing and others. There are also relaxation and keep-fit classes, many of which cater specially for older people.

The national organisations below can put you in touch with local groups. Your library and adult education centre should also be helpful.

English Folk Dance and Song Society, Cecil Sharp House, 2 Regent's Park Road, London NW1 7AY. T:0171 485 2206. Has about 570 clubs nationwide. Membership costs £21 (£11 for over 60s).

Imperial Society of Teachers of Dancing, Imperial House, 22-26 Paul Street, London EC2A 4QE. T:0171 377 1577. Can provide names of local teachers, many of whom organise classes especially for older people.

Keep Fit Association, Francis House, Francis Street, London SW1P 1DE. T:0171 233 8898. The KFA offers 'Fitness through Movement, Exercise and Dance' classes, suitable for all ages and abilities. Almost all adult education centres run classes, many specially geared to keeping fit in retirement.

Royal Scottish Country Dance Society, 12 Coates Crescent, Edinburgh EH3 7AF. T:0131 225 3854. The Society has members from 16 to 80-plus in its many branches and groups all over the world.

For people with disabilities

Happily, there are increasingly fewer activities from which people with disabilities are debarred through lack of suitable facilities. This section deals with one topic not covered elsewhere, namely enjoyment of books.

Calibre, Aylesbury, Bucks HP22 5XQ. T:01296 432339 (24-hour service). Lends recorded books on standard cassettes to anyone with a doctor's certificate certifying their 'inability to read printed books in the normal way'. There are some 4,000 titles, including fiction and non-fiction.

National Library for the Blind, Far Cromwell Road, Bredbury, Stockport, Cheshire SK6 2SG. T:0161 494 0217 (24 hours). Lends books and music scores in Braille and Moon free of charge (also post-free).

RNIB Talking Book Service, Mount Pleasant, Wembley, Middx HA0 1RR. T:0181 903 6666. This is a library service with more than 10,000 titles for anyone who cannot easily read normal print. The charge is normally paid by members' local authorities. Special recorder machines are available on permanent loan.

Games

Many local areas have their own bridge, chess, whist, dominoes, Scrabble and other groups who meet to enjoy friendly games. Your library should have details. Or, you can contact the national organisations below.

British Chess Federation, 9a Grand Parade, St. Leonards on Sea, East Sussex TN38 ODD. T:01424 442500.

English Bridge Union, Broadfields, Bicester Road, Aylesbury, Bucks HP19 3BG. T:01296 394414.

Scrabble Clubs UK, Richard House, Enstone Road, Enfield, Middx EN3 7TB. T:0181 805 4848.

Gardens and gardening

Gardens to visit, special help for people with disabilities, how to run a gardening association ... the organisations listed will be able to advise.

Gardening for the Disabled Trust & Garden Club, Hayes Farmhouse, Hayes Lane, Peasmarsh, Nr Rye, East Sussex TN31 6XR. Provides practical and financial help to disabled people who want to garden actively. The annual subscription is £3.

Horticultural Therapy, Goulds Ground, Vallis Way, Frome, Somerset BA11 3DW. T:01373 464782. Helps elderly, disabled or visually impaired people to garden. There is an advisory service; also demonstrations, workshops and meetings.

National Gardens Scheme, Hatchlands Park, East Clandon, Guildford, Surrey GU4 7RT. T:01483 211535. (For England and Wales.) The Scheme covers nearly 3,500 private gardens which are open to the public, perhaps one day a year, to raise money for charity. Further information is given in the Scheme's Yellow Book, *The Gardens of England and Wales* (£3.50 from booksellers). The organisation is always looking for new gardens. Should you wish to offer yours, however small, apply to the county organiser (see handbook for address).

National Society of Allotment and Leisure Gardeners Ltd., O'Dell House, Hunters Road, Corby, Northants NN17 5JE. T:01536 266576. The Society encourages all forms of horticultural education and the forming of local allotment and gardening associations. Membership gives you access to free advice plus receipt of the Society's bulletin.

Royal Horticultural Society, PO Box 313, Vincent Square, London SW1P 2PE. T:0171 821 3000. Members receive free tickets to 24 gardens and privileged tickets to shows, including the Chelsea Flower Show. They can also attend lectures and demonstrations throughout the UK. Membership costs £25 (plus a one-off enrolment fee of £7). For further information, contact the Membership Manager.

History

People with an interest in the past have a truly glorious choice of activities to sample.

Age Exchange Reminiscence Centre, 11 Blackheath Village, Blackheath, London SE3 9LA. T:0181 318 9105. The Centre features exhibitions recording the life-styles of the 1920s and 1930s. There are also publications plus a year-round programme of activities including music and drama. Admission free.

City of London Information Centre, St. Paul's Churchyard (South side), London EC4M 8BX. T:0171 332 1456. The City of London offers enough interest to occupy you for a year or longer. The Centre gives advice and guidance and has lots of free leaflets.

English Heritage (Membership Department), PO Box 1BB, London W1A 1BB. T:0171 973 3400. Manages many historic properties. Members receive a Welcome Pack, a card granting free admission plus a magazine. Annual subscription is £23, £14.50 for senior citizens.

Federation of Family History Societies, The Benson Room, Birmingham and Midland Institute, Margaret Street, Birmingham B3 3BS. An umbrella organisation for 190 societies throughout the world (130 in the UK) that provide assistance if you are interested in tracing your ancestors. Write to Mrs Pauline Saul, enclosing (A4) sae.

Friends of Historic Scotland, Longmore House, Salisbury Place, Edinburgh EH9 1SH. T:0131 668 8999. Membership gives you free access to historic buildings and ancient monuments, special guided tours and a quarterly magazine. Membership is £18 a year; less for senior citizens.

Historical Association, 59a Kennington Park Road, London SE11 4JH. T:0171 735 3901. Members enjoy a wide variety of activities such as lectures, conferences and conducted tours. There are over 70 local branches. Membership costs £25 a year.

Historic Houses Association (Membership), PO Box 21, Heritage House, Baldock, Herts SG7 5SH. Friends of the HHA enjoy free entrance to nearly 300 HHA-member houses and gardens and receive invitations to concerts, receptions and other events. Membership costs £28.

National Trust, 36 Queen Anne's Gate, London SW1H 9AS. T:0181 315 1111. Exists to protect historic buildings and areas of great natural beauty. Membership gives you free entry to the Trust's many properties. Hundreds of special events are arranged each year. Membership costs £27.

Hobbies

Most of the organisations listed arrange events, answer queries and can put you in contact with kindred spirits.

The British Association of Numismatic Societies, Secretary: P H Mernick, c/o Bush Boake Allen Ltd., Blackhorse Lane, London E17 5QP. An umbrella organisation for some 60 local clubs for those interested in the study or collection of coins.

British Jigsaw Puzzle Library, 8 Heath Terrace, Leamington Spa, Warwickshire CV32 5LY. T:01926 311874. This is a lending library with puzzles usually exchanged by post. Subscriptions range from £27 for three months to £65 for a year. Postal charges are extra.

National Association of Flower Arrangement Societies, 21 Denbigh Street, London SW1V 2HF. T:0171 828 5145. Can put you in touch with local clubs and classes.

National Philatelic Society, 107 Charterhouse Street, London EC1M 6PT. T:0171 336 0882. Holds monthly Saturday meetings, usually including an auction. Members receive a journal and there is also an exchange packet scheme. Membership costs £21 a year.

The Royal Photographic Society, The Octagon, Milsom Street, Bath BA1 1DN. T:01225 462841. Arranges lectures, workshops, exhibitions, field trips and social events. Membership costs £75; £55 for over 65s.

Museums

Most museums organise free lectures and guided tours. As with art galleries and theatres, an increasing trend is to form a group of 'Friends' who pay a membership subscription to support the museum and in return enjoy certain advantages, such as: access to private views, receptions and other social activities. Examples include:

British Museum Society, The British Museum, London WC1B 3DG. T:0171 323 8605.

Friends of the Fitzwilliam Muesum, Fitzwilliam Museum, Trumpington Street, Cambridge CB2 1RB. T:01223 332900.

Friends of the National Maritime Museum, Greenwich, London SE10 9NF. T:0181 312 6678/6638.

Museum of the Moving Image, South Bank, London SE1 8XT. T:0171 401 2636 (recorded information).

Friends of the National Museums of Scotland, The Royal Museum of Scotland, Chambers Street, Edinburgh EH1 1JF. T:0131 225 7534.

Friends of the V & A, The Victoria and Albert Museum, London SW7 2RL. T:0171 589 4040.

Nature and conservation

The potential list is enormous. To give you a flavour, herewith a short 'mixed bag'. See also 'The Fun and Challenge of Voluntary Work' chapter.

Amenity organisations. You should be able to contact your local society through your public library.

The Civic Trust, 17 Carlton House Terrace, London SW1Y 5AW. T:0171 930 0914. Acts as an umbrella organisation for nearly 1,000 local amenity groups and publishes a quarterly newsletter with articles on planning, conservation and transport issues. Annual subscription £12.

Forestry Commission, 231 Corstorphine Road, Edinburgh EH12 7AT. T:0131 334 0303. For information on walks, picnic places and visitor centres contact your local Forestry Commission office or the Information Branch at the above address.

The Royal Society for the Protection of Birds, The Lodge, Sandy, Bedfordshire SG19 2DL. T:01767 680551. Acts to protect wild birds and the places in which they breed. Members enjoy free entry to 140 nature reserves. There is also a national network of local groups. Membership is £22.

The Wildlife Trusts, The Green, Witham Park, Waterside South, Lincoln LN5 7JR. T:01522 544400. There are some 150 local Trusts and Groups which between them care for 2,000 nature reserves. By joining the Trust for your area, you can visit the reserves, enjoy guided walks, talks and other events. Application forms for membership (£16) from the above address.

Public library service

Britain's public library service is among the best in the world. It issues about 600 million books a year, loans records and cassettes and is a source of vast amount of information.

Many libraries have a mobile service and some also have volunteer library visitors who deliver books and materials to housebound people. Large print books are usually available as are musical scores, leaflets on DSS benefits, consumer information and details of local activities.

Sport

Retirement is an ideal time to get into trim. Facilities abound and, unlike people with a 9 to 5 job, you enjoy the great advantage of being able to book out of peak hours. To find out about opportunities in your area, contact your local authority recreational department, your sports/leisure centre or the regional office of the English Sports Council, address from: The Information Centre, **English Sports Council**, 16 Upper Woburn Place, London WC1H 0QP. T:0171 273 1700.

Also useful to know about is: **The Central Council of Physical Recreation**, Francis House, Francis Street, London SW1P 1DE. T:0171 828 3163/4. They can give information and advice on all types of sport.

Angling

The Angling Foundation, Federation House, National Agricultural Centre, Stoneleigh Park, Warwickshire CV8 2RF. T:01203 414999. Can advise on where to find qualified tuition, local tackle dealers and similar information.

Archery

Grand National Archery Society, 7th Street, The National Agricultural Centre, Stoneleigh, Kenilworth, Warwickshire CV8 2LG. T:01203 696631. Can put you in touch with your nearest club of which there are now over 1,200 around the country.

Badminton

Badminton Association of England Ltd., National Badminton Centre, Bradwell Road, Loughton Lodge, Milton Keynes, Bucks MK8 9LA. T:01908 568822. Most sports centres have badminton courts and give instruction, as do many Adult Education Institutes. If you need advice, or are interested in a short residential course, contact the Association.

Bowling

There are many clubs all over the country. For addresses contact:

English Bowling Association, Lyndhurst Road, Worthing, West Sussex BN11 2AZ. T:01903 820222.

English Women's Bowling Association, 2 Case Gardens, Seaton, Devon EX12 2AP. T:01297 21317.

English Indoor Bowling Association, David Cornwell House, Bowling Green, Leicester Road, Melton Mowbray, Leics LE13 0DA. T:01664 481900.

Clay pigeon shooting

Clay Pigeon Shooting Association, Earlstrees Court, Earlstrees Road, Corby, Northants NN17 4AY. T:01536 443566. As a member you have public liability insurance, your scores are recorded in the national averages and you can compete in national events. Annual membership is £25; £20 for veterans (60 and over).

Cricket

Lord's Cricket Ground, St. John's Wood Road, London NW8 8QN. T:0171 432 1033. You can enjoy a conducted tour of Lord's. Price is £5.50 (£4 for pensioners). Tour times (normally noon and 2 p.m.) sometimes vary, so check before making a special visit. Half-price tickets are available to pensioners for some matches.

England and Wales Cricket Board, Lord's Cricket Ground, London NW8 8QZ. T:0171 432 1200. If you want to play, watch or help at cricket matches, contact your local club or send an sae to the above address.

Croquet

Croquet Association, Paul Campion, Secretary, The Hurlingham Club, Ranelagh Gardens, London SW6 3PR. T:0171 736 3148.

Many local authorities offer facilities for croquet enthusiasts. The Association runs coaching courses and can advise about clubs, membership, events and purchase of equipment.

Cycling

Cyclists' Touring Club, Cotterell House, 69 Meadrow, Godalming, Surrey GU7 3HS. T:01483 417217. The CTC offers members free third party insurance, free legal aid, a handbook, organised cycling holidays and introductions to 200 local cycling groups. Membership costs £25 a year; £16.50 for retired people.

Darts

British Darts Organisation Ltd., 2 Pages Lane, Muswell Hill, London N10 1PS. T:0181 883 5544/5. Opportunities for playing darts can be found almost anywhere in clubs, pubs and sports centres. Contact the national body should you require further help.

Golf

English Golf Union, The Broadway, Woodhall Spa, Lincs LN10 6PU. T:01526 354500.

Golfing Union of Ireland, Glencar House, 81 Eglinton Road, Donnybrook, Dublin 4. T:00 353 1 2694111.

Scottish Golf Union, Scottish National Golf Centre, Drumoig, Leuchars, St. Andrews, Fife KY16 0DW. T:01382 549500.

Welsh Golfing Union, Catsash, Newport, Gwent NP6 1JQ. T:01633 430830.

The National Golf Unions can provide information about municipal courses and private clubs. Additionally many adult education institutes and sports centres run classes for beginners.

Rambling

Ramblers' Association, 1-5 Wandsworth Road, London SW8 2XX. T:0171 339 8500. Will be glad to put you in touch with one of its many local groups. Membership is £17 a year; £8.50 when retired.

Swimming

Amateur Swimming Association, Harold Fern House, Derby Square, Loughborough, Leics LE11 5AL. T:01509 618700. Classes are arranged by many authorities who also make the pool available at various times of the week for older people who prefer to swim quietly. The Association offers many award schemes as an incentive to swim regularly for fitness and health. Further details on request from the ASA.

Table tennis

The **Veterans English Table Tennis Society (VETTS)**, Harwood House, 90 Broadway, Letchworth, Herts SG6 3PH. T:01462 671191. Holds regional and national championships including singles and doubles events for over 40s, 50s, 60s and 70s. Annual membership is £10; £5 for those over 65.

Tennis

Veterans' Lawn Tennis Association of Great Britain, c/o Valerie Willoughby, 26 Marryat Square, London SW6 6UA. Promotes competitions for 'veterans' in various age groups. The VLTA Yearbook (£2) lists affiliated clubs.

Yachting

Royal Yachting Association, RYA House, Romsey Road, Eastleigh, Hampshire SO50 9YA. T:01703 627400. There are 1,500 sailing clubs affiliated to the RYA and more than 1,000 recognised teaching establishments. Membership costs £17 a year.

Women's organisations

Although today women can participate in almost any activity on equal terms with men, women's clubs and organisations continue to enjoy enormous popularity. Among the best known are Women's Institutes, the Mothers' Union and Townswomen's Guilds.

Mothers' Union, 24 Tufton Street, London SW1P 3RB. T:0171 222 5533. Members are involved in a wide range of activities which balance service to the community, learning, worship and recreation. Housebound members are linked through prayer circles.

National Association of Women's Clubs, 5 Vernon Rise, King's Cross Road, London WC1X 9EP. T:0171 837 1434. Typical activities include: crafts, health care, music, drama and keep fit. Membership is £4.50 a year to head office plus a small membership fee to the local club.

National Federation of Women's Institutes, 104 New Kings Road, London SW6 4LY. T:0171 371 9300. The WI offers women the opportunity to improve the quality of life and to develop individual skills and talents. There is a college, which runs short courses and also a monthly magazine. Membership is £13 per annum.

Women in Scotland and Northern Ireland should contact:

Scottish Women's Rural Institutes, 42 Heriot Row, Edinburgh EH3 6ES. T:0131 225 1724.

Federation of Women's Institutes of Northern Ireland, 209-211 Upper Lisburn Road, Belfast BT10 0LL. T:01232 301506.

Townswomen's Guilds, Chamber of Commerce House, 75 Harborne Road, Edgbaston, Birmingham B15 3DA. T:0121 456 3435. The Guilds have around 80,000 members who meet to exchange ideas, learn new skills, take part in a wide range of local activities – and have fun. Annual subscription is £9.50.

Public Transport. One of the big gains of reaching retirement age is the availability of cheap travel. Most local authorities offer concessionary fares to senior citizens during the off-peak periods. Coaches too very often have special rates for older people and, as everyone knows, Senior Railcards, available to men and women over 60, offer wonderful savings.

9

The Fun and Challenge of Voluntary Work

Many people find immense satisfaction through becoming involved in some form of voluntary work. The choice of possibilities is enormous and your contribution will be greatly appreciated.

If you have a special field of interest, such as children, you could find ideas by looking under the relevant heading further in the chapter. Alternatively, the following organisations will be able to advise, tell you what openings exist locally and point you in the right direction.

REACH, Bear Wharf, 27 Bankside, London SE1 9ET. T:0171 928 0452. Specialises in placing retired people with business or other professional skills in voluntary organisations. All jobs are unpaid but with out-of-pocket expenses met.

Scottish Corps of Retired Executives, sponsored by Scottish Business in the Community, Romano House, 43 Station Road, Edinburgh EH12 7AF. T:0131 334 9876. Assists charities, community organisations and small businesses. Members are retired business people who give what time they can spare. Contact the Administrator.

The National Centre for Volunteering, Carriage Row, 183 Eversholt Street, London NW1 1BU. T:0171 388 9888. Can advise if you want to volunteer for the first time and can also help with information about volunteer opportunities in your area.

Volunteer Bureaux. Usually listed in the telephone book under 'V'. Most towns have a body of this kind which seeks to match volunteers with local organisations. Alternatively, see the *Volunteer Bureaux Directory,* available at most libraries.

Citizens' Advice Bureau. Your local CAB will also have information on local needs and groups to contact.

General

The scope of the work of the British Red Cross, WRVS and Citizens' Advice Bureau is so broad that they almost justify a category to themselves.

British Red Cross (BRCS), 9 Grosvenor Crescent, London SW1X 7EJ. T:0171 235 5454. The Red Cross needs help from men and women for first aid, community care and welfare services. Training is always given. It also needs fund-raisers, publicity officers and drivers for escort work.

Expenses are paid. Contact the local branch (under 'British' or 'Red Cross' in the telephone book) or write to the National Volunteer Co-ordinator at the national headquarters above.

Women's Royal Voluntary Service, Milton Hill House, Milton Hill, Abingdon, Oxon OX13 6AF. T:01235 442900. The WRVS works with the local authority Social Services to cover almost the complete range of needs in the community. It particularly welcomes offers of help from people with time during the working day.

Activities include: meals on wheels, home support for elderly people, organising children's holiday schemes, running hospital shops and assisting with welfare services in emergencies.

Citizens' Advice Bureaux deal with over 7 million enquiries a year. Apart from being an excellent source of information about other volunteer openings, the CAB itself has over 15,000 volunteer helpers working in its many branches throughout the country.

The work involves advising clients on a wide range of questions from welfare benefits to local community schemes. No formal qualifications are required but applicants must be able to master a considerable amount of detailed information.

Training is given and volunteers are expected to work a minimum of six hours a week in their Bureau. Contact the Manager of your nearest CAB for information.

Another organisation to know about is: **Community Service Volunteers**, 237 Pentonville Road, London N1 9NJ. T:0171 278 6601. It operates a nationwide scheme called the Retired and Senior Volunteer Programme (RSVP) for people aged over 50 who want to be involved in their community. Each group plans its own activities which might include working with elderly people, advising young people starting out on their own and going into schools to support teachers. Contact Janet Atfield.

Animals

Cinnamon Trust, Foundry House, Foundry Square, Hayle, Cornwall TR27 4HH. T:01736 757900. Seeks to help elderly pet owners who, owing to some emergency, are temporarily unable to care for their pets.

Animal lovers throughout the country assist either by fostering a pet in their own home or helping out on a daily basis, for example walking a dog or cleaning out a bird cage. Long-term homes are also required for pets who have lost their owners. For further details, write to Mrs. Averil Jarvis at the above address (enclosing sae).

Pet Fostering Service Scotland. T: 01877 331496. Provides a similar service in Scotland. If you have a love of pets and would like to help out in a crisis, telephone the above number.

PRO Dogs, Rocky Bank, 4 New Road, Ditton, Maidstone, Kent ME20 6AD. T:01732 848499. PRO Dogs is a national charity which originated the PAT Dog Hospital visiting scheme. Dog owners visit hospital wards and residential homes with their pets to give people in institutional care an outlet for affection. An essential is that the dogs are of suitable temperament and well behaved. To participate, it is necessary to become a PRO Dogs member to be covered by their insurance scheme. Annual subscription is £10.

Royal Society for the Prevention of Cruelty to Animals, Causeway, Horsham, West Sussex RH12 1HG. T:01403 264181. Volunteers are needed to help with fund-raising. Contact headquarters for the address of your nearest branch.

Bereavement

Cruse Bereavement Care, Cruse House, 126 Sheen Road, Richmond, Surrey TW9 1UR. T:0181 940 4818. Cruse is the national organisation for people who have been bereaved. It provides counselling, practical help and organises social programmes. Volunteers are needed in the branch offices to help in all these ways.

Children and young people

Action for Sick Children, Argyle House, 29 31 Euston Road, London NW1 2SD. T:0171 833 2041. Local branches give practical help to sick children and their families including: providing transport to hospital; helping with volunteer play schemes on the wards and fund-raising to provide more parents' and children's facilities in hospital. Contact HQ for address of local branch.

Barnardo's, Tanners Lane, Barkingside, Ilford, Essex IG6 1QG. T:0181 550 8822. Barnardo's provides many imaginative services for disadvantaged children. There are two ways you can help: by fund-raising (write to the National Volunteer Development Manager); and by supporting the Child Care Programme. This usually involves befriending a young person with a disability, perhaps to give the mother a much-needed break (write to the Information Officer).

Children's Country Holidays Fund, 1st Floor (Rear), 42-43 Lower Marsh, Tanswell Street, London SE1 7RG. T:0171 928 6522. Contact: The Chief Executive. The purpose is to give disadvan-taged London children a country holiday, either in private homes or camps. Host families are needed as are London organisers, camp supervisors and train marshals.

Save the Children, Mary Datchelor House, 17 Grove Lane, London SE5 8RD. T:0171 703 5400. Requires help both in their shops and with fund-raising.

Scout Association, Baden-Powell House, Queen's Gate, London SW7 5JS. T:0171 584 7030. Volunteers are needed to help with: organising events, training (e.g. vehicle maintenance and map reading), editing newsletters and much else.

Sea Cadet Corps, 202 Lambeth Road, London SE1 7JF. T:0171 928 8978. Offers boys and girls aged 12-18 challenging new experiences and adventure. Units throughout the UK welcome volunteer help either as administrators or specialist instructors. Contact the national headquarters.

The Children's Society, Edward Rudolf House, Margery Street, London WC1X 0JL. T:0171 837 4299. It runs over 90 projects which include refuges for young runaways, family centres and respite care for young people with disabilities. Help is needed in the Society's charity shops, as is fund-raising.

Volunteer Reading Help, 4th Floor, High Holborn House, 52/54 High Holborn, London WC1V 6RL. T:0171 404 6204. The purpose is to assist children aged 6 to 11 who need encouragement with their reading. Volunteers spare two hours, twice a week during term time, by going into a local school and giving individual attention to three children on a regular basis. No formal qualifications are needed but volunteers must have plenty of patience and be willing to commit themselves for at least a year. A short training is provided. The scheme covers around a quarter of primary schools in England. For further information, if you would like to help, telephone the National Office above.

Conservation

BTCV (British Trust for Conservation Volunteers), 36 St. Mary's Street, Wallingford, Oxfordshire OX10 0EU. T:01491 839766. Over 1,900 local groups run community projects including: planting trees, cleaning ponds, creating urban nature areas, restoring footpaths and protecting valuable habitats for wildlife. There is also a full programme of working holidays.

Council for the Protection of Rural England (CPRE), Warwick House, 25 Buckingham Palace Road, London SW1W 0PP. T:0171 976 6433. Volunteers act as local watchdogs, reporting threats to the environment and sometimes representing the Council at enquiries. Fund-raising is also always needed.

Friends of the Earth, 26-28 Underwood Street, London N1 7JQ. T:0171 490 1555. Over 250 groups run local campaigns and fund-raising projects. These can be contacted through the London office where help with the administration is much welcomed.

Greenpeace, Canonbury Villas, London N1 2PN. T:0171 865 8100. A pressure group which campaigns to protect the environment against pollution. Volunteers are needed both to help in the London office and also for campaigning by local groups across the country.

Ramblers' Association, 1-5 Wandsworth Road, London SW8 2XX. T:0171 339 8500. Aims to keep footpaths open and to protect the countryside. Its 50 area offices need help with administration and with checking the condition of the local footpaths.

Scottish Conservation Projects Trust, Balallan House, 24 Allan Park, Stirling FK8 2QG. T:01786 479697. SCP runs 7-14 day conservation projects in all parts of Scotland as well as weekend and single day events. Type of work varies from conservation proper – fencing, footpath construction and habitat management – to jobs such as office skills and fund-raising. Individuals pay their own fares, plus a contribution to board and lodging (£4 a day). Annual membership is £15 (£8 for pensioners). For further information, contact SCP at the above address.

The elderly

Abbeyfield Society, 53 Victoria Street, St. Albans, Herts AL1 3UW. T:01727 857536. Builds houses to provide independent accommodation for older people who are on their own and also residential care schemes for those who can no longer look after themselves. Volunteers assist in many ways: e.g. shopping, gardening, typing, fund-raising or advising on the purchase of new Abbeyfield houses.

Age Concern England, Astral House, 1268 London Road, London SW16 4ER. T:0181 679 8000; **Age Concern Scotland,** 113 Rose Street, Edinburgh EH2 3DT, T:0131 220 3345; **Age Concern Cymru,** 4th Floor, 1 Cathedral Road, Cardiff CF1 9SD, T:01222 371566; **Age Concern Northern Ireland,** 3 Lower Crescent, Belfast BT7 1NR. T:01232 245729.

Age Concern promotes the welfare of older people. Local groups, using volunteer helpers, provide such services as day care, lunch clubs, home visiting and over 60s' clubs. For addresses, contact the central offices listed above.

Carers National Association, 20-25 Glasshouse Yard, London EC1A 4JS. T:0171 490 8818. Helps those who care for elderly or infirm people at home. It provides an advisory service, campaigns for better benefits and supports holiday help for carers. Assistance is needed with carers' groups, to enable them to meet occasionally. Contact the Information Department for details of your local branch.

Contact the Elderly, 15 Henrietta Street, Covent Garden, London WC2E 8QH. Freephone: 0800 716543. Offers a way of making new friends and of providing companionship for lonely elderly people. Volunteers escort them once a month to enjoy tea in someone's home. Help is needed with driving (one Sunday a month) and/or hosting a tea-party for about 10 people once or twice a year. No expenses are paid. Ring the above number for name of local organiser.

Help the Aged, St. James's Walk, London EC1R 0BE. T:0171 253 0253. Funds day centres, community transport, home safety devices, emergency alarm systems and sheltered housing. Volunteer help is needed to staff charity shops and to assist local organisers. Contact the Volunteer Co-ordinator.

The family

Marriage Care, Clitherow House, 1 Blythe Mews, Blythe Road,

London W14 0NW. T:0171 371 1341. Runs pre-marriage courses and a counselling service for anyone with relationship problems. Help is needed in administering its 80 centres. New potential counsellors are also sought. For local addresses, contact the headquarters above.

Relate, Herbert Gray College, Little Church Street, Rugby, Warwickshire CV21 3AP. T:01788 573241. Volunteers who would like to become counsellors receive training. The work is most likely to appeal to people with some background in social or community activity.

SSAFA Forces Help (formerly SSAFA and the Forces Help Society), 19 Queen Elizabeth Street, London SE1 2LP. T:0171 403 8783. Volunteers in over 100 UK branches deal with every kind of problem – domestic, financial, legal and compassionate. Training is given and although there is no minimum time commitment it is critical to see a case through to the end. Help is particularly needed in inner cities. A service background may be helpful but is not necessary.

Health and disability

British Ski Club for the Disabled, Springmount, Berwick St. John, Shaftesbury, Dorset SP7 0HQ. T:01747 828515. Its aim is to encourage people with a disability to learn or continue to enjoy the fun of skiing and the self-confidence gained from participating in an exhilarating sport. Volunteers, who must be competent parallel skiers, are needed to act as teachers and guides both on artificial slopes around the country and skiing holidays abroad. The Club runs its own instructor courses. Small subsidies are available for guides on authorised holiday parties.

Calibre, Cassette Library for the Blind and Print Disabled, Aylesbury, Bucks HP22 5XQ. T:01296 432339 or 81211. Volunteers are needed to help run the library and also to assist with publicity and fund-raising. Contact the General Secretary.

Cancer Research Campaign, 10 Cambridge Terrace, London NW1 4JL. T:0171 224 1333. Supports research at centres throughout the UK with the aim of defeating cancer. Money for this is raised by local committees and hundreds of honorary organisers. If you would like to help, see telephone directory for the address of your local group.

Imperial Cancer Research Fund, 61 Lincoln's Inn Fields, London

WC2A 3PX. T:0171 242 0200. Funds one-third of all cancer research in the UK. Help is needed in shops (sorting, serving, ironing, mending and similar) or to assist with office work in the Regional Centres. See *Yellow Pages* for number of your nearest Centre.

Leonard Cheshire Foundation, 26-29 Maunsel Street, London SW1P 2QN. T:0171 828 1822. Works for the care and rehabilitation of people with physical, mental or learning disabilities. All its homes and services are supported by local volunteers, who make a huge contribution.

There are endless practical ways you might help: driving, gardening, decorating, shopping and fund-raising. The London office will give you the address of the nearest home.

MENCAP, Holiday Services, 119 Drake Street, Rochdale OL16 1PZ. T:01706 54111. Volunteers help on holidays for unaccompanied children and for adults with learning disabilities. Board and lodging is free and a small travel allowance is paid.

Mind (The Mental Health Charity), Granta House, 15-19 Broadway, London E15 4BQ. T:0181 519 2122. Works to promote the interests of mentally ill people. The local associations (see telephone directory) vary in the scope of their work. While all will be involved in fund-raising, their activities also include running social clubs and day centres as well as giving support to individuals.

National Association of Leagues of Hospital Friends, 2nd Floor, Fairfax House, Causton Road, Colchester, Essex CO1 1RJ. T:01206 761227. Each League is autonomous and opportunities for voluntary work vary. All, however, are concerned with both service to patients and fund-raising and all need volunteers. The National Association can put new volunteers in touch with their local League.

National Back Pain Association, 16 Elmtree Road, Teddington, Middlesex TW11 8ST. T:0181 977 5474. The NBPA needs volunteers in their local branches to give practical help to back pain sufferers. Activities include: organising exercise and hydrotherapy classes, arranging talks and running social and fund-raising events. For further information, contact the Branches Officer.

Riding for the Disabled Association, Avenue R, National Agricultural Centre, Kenilworth, Warwickshire CV8 2LY. T:01703 696510. Provides opportunities for riding for disabled children and adults. You do not have to be horsey to help with the administration or fund-raising in one of the 700 local groups. For those with experience of horses, the main jobs are leading or walking beside the ponies and accompanying parties on riding holidays. Contact the head office for address of your nearest group.

Royal National Institute for the Blind, 224 Great Portland Street, London W1N 6AA. T:0171 388 1266. RNIB aims to help blind and partially sighted people lead full and independent lives. Help is mostly required with fund-raising. Volunteers are also needed all over the country to service talking book players, two or three times a month. London office will put you in touch with your nearest group.

St. John Ambulance, 1 Grosvenor Crescent, London SW1X 7EF. T:0171 235 5231. Best known for their first aid role at public events, St. John Ambulance volunteers also help with such activities as vehicle maintenance, fund-raising, public relations and community care. For information contact your county office or the national headquarters above.

SCOPE (formerly the Spastics Society), 12 Park Crescent, London W1N 4EQ. T:0171 636 5020. Contact the Information Officer. There are over 200 local groups. Helpers are needed particularly for driving, running open days, helping in the shops and with fund-raising and street collections.

Sue Ryder Foundation, Sue Ryder Home, Cavendish, Sudbury, Suffolk CO10 8AY. T:01787 280252. Contact: Mr K Wilkinson. Their homes cater for the sick and disabled of all ages. Volunteers are needed for a variety of jobs including help with the general running of the homes. Those with secretarial skills are particularly sought for weekend work. Board and lodging is provided.

Heritage and the arts

Arts Council of England, Information Department, 14 Great Peter Street, London SW1P 3NQ. T:0171 333 0100. There is attractive scope for becoming involved in the arts in a volunteer capacity. All kinds of abilities are needed from painting and other creative talents to accounting, clerical know-how, marketing and communications skills. Ask at the library for address of your local arts council.

National Trust, 33 Sheep Street, Cirencester, Glos GL7 1QW. T:01285 651818. Volunteers are involved in many aspects of the Trust's work in conserving the great houses open to the public as well as coast and countryside properties. Write to the Volunteers Officer.

There is also a programme of working holidays in outdoor conservation. For details, send large sae with two first class stamps to: **The National Trust Working Holidays**, PO Box 84, Cirencester, Glos GL7 1ZP.

The needy

DGAA Homelife, 1 Derry Street, London W8 5HY. T:0171 369 6700. Assists people from professional or similar backgrounds either financially or with care in residential homes. Work involves visiting patients and helping to organise outings for them; also fund-raising.

Oxfam, Oxfam House, 274 Banbury Road, Oxford OX2 7DZ. T:0800 601010. Volunteers help with the running of Oxfam shops, organise fund-raising events, give administrative help and support the educational aspect of Oxfam's work. For further information, contact your local Oxfam shop or office (see telephone directory) or ring the above number.

Royal British Legion, Poppy Appeal, Aylesford, Kent ME20 7NX. T:01622 717172. Best known for its Poppy Day Appeal, the Royal British Legion also runs care homes, maintains sheltered workshops, organises training, gives pension counselling and offers friendship through its many branches.

Its most pressing need is to recruit more Poppy Appeal organisers and volunteers for street, or house-to-house, collections. If you would like to help with the Appeal, contact Pat Reger at the above address. If you would like to help in other ways, T:0345 725725.

The Samaritans, 10 The Grove, Slough, Berks SL1 1QP. T:01753 532713. The Samaritans offer emotional support to the suicidal and the despairing. Much of the work is done on the telephone so that, while no special qualifications are required, good hearing, an unshockable disposition and complete reliability are essential qualities in a volunteer. Training is given. The minimum time commitment is about 12 hours a month plus a few all-night duties each year.

Work with ex-offenders

NACRO (National Association for the Care and Resettlement of Offenders), 169 Clapham Road, London SW9 0PU. T:0171 582

6500. Opportunities for voluntary work are organised locally and include such projects as arranging education for unemployed adults and running activities for young people. For further details, contact Information Enquiries.

Society of Voluntary Associates (SOVA), 350 Kennington Road, London SE11 4LH. T:0171 793 0404. Promotes the work of volunteers with offenders, their families and young people at risk. The work may be with children, in the adult literacy scheme, prison visiting or helping ex-offenders. Training is given by SOVA and the volunteer then works in a Probation Service or Befrienders' Scheme.

Useful reading

A Guide for Absolute Beginners. Booklet for people with business or professional skills interested in voluntary work. Free from: REACH, Bear Wharf, 27 Bankside, London SE1 9ET.

The Spirit of Volunteering, free from: The National Centre for Volunteering, Carriage Row, 183 Eversholt Street, London NW1 1BU.

Directory of Volunteering and Employment Opportunities. Price £9.95 from Directory of Social Change, 24 Stephenson Way, London NW1 2DP.

10

Looking After Your Health

How often have you commented when meeting a recently retired friend: 'Goodness, he looks a different man. Fit, relaxed, contented – retirement must suit him.' And why not? Perhaps more than any other period since your twenties, retirement is a time for positive good health! You have more chance to be out in the fresh air and take up a favourite sport again. Also, once free of the strains and pressures that are part of any job, you will feel less harassed, look better and, best of all, have the energy to devote to new interests and activities.

Keeping fit

Exercise plays an important part in keeping you healthy. It tones up muscles, improves the circulation, reduces flab, helps ward off illnesses such as heart disease and, above all, can be a great deal of fun.

The experts' motto is: little and often. For those not accustomed to regular exercise, it is essential to build up gradually.

Training in a wide range of sports is available around the country – with many sessions especially focused on the over-fifties.

As well as some of the more exotic choices, swimming has long been recognised as one of the best forms of exercise. Some swear that there is nothing to beat a good brisk walk.

Gardening is also recommended. With the explosion of leisure centres and keep fit classes run by local authorities, opportunities have never been better for athletes of all ability levels – and none.

Opportunities for more leisurely keep fit are also on the increase with plenty of options for older people. The town hall should be able to tell you what exists locally. The following organisations may also be able to help.

Extend, 22 Maltings Drive, Wheathampstead, Herts AL4 8QJ. T:01582 832760. Provides recreational movement sessions to music, especially for the over-sixties and people with disabilities. For information about classes in your area please enclose stamps to the value of £2.

Health and Beauty Exercise, 52 London Street, Chertsey, Surrey KT16 8AJ. T:01932 564567. A national organisation that runs movement and exercise-to-music classes, with some participants aged 70 and older. Membership (including joining fee) is about £5. Classes cost from about £1.50 to £3.

Relaxation for Living Trust, Foxhills, 30 Victoria Avenue, Shanklin, IOW, PO37 6LS. T: 01983 868166. A main aim is teaching how to manage stress. There are usually between six and ten in a class. For list of local classes, please send large sae.

Yoga

Around half a million people in Britain regularly practise yoga as a means of improving fitness and helping relaxation. Many local authorities run classes. Herewith also three specialist organisations which arrange courses in many parts of the country:

British Wheel of Yoga, 1 Hamilton Place, Boston Road, Sleaford, Lincs NG34 7ES. T:01529 306851.

Iyengar Yoga Institute, 223a Randolph Avenue, London W9 1NL. T:0171 624 3080.

Yoga for Health Foundation, Ickwell Bury, Biggleswade, Beds SG18 9EF. T:01767 627271.

Sensible eating

A trim, well kept body is one of the secrets of a youthful appearance, whereas being fat and out-of-condition adds years to anyone's age. Regular exercise is one-half of the equation, sensible eating the other. Not to put too fine a point on it, more than one in five adults in Britain is obese – in other words, overweight. No one is going to fuss about two or three pounds but half a stone or more, as well as looking unsightly, starts to become a health risk. In middle-aged men in particular, it increases the possibility of a heart attack, makes operations more difficult – and, in older people, is one of the causes of restricted mobility.

No one should go on a serious diet without first consulting their doctor. Medical advice is not necessary for knocking off. sweets, cakes, sticky buns, deep-fried foods, alcohol and rich sauces.

As a rule chubby people tend to be those who enjoy rather too many good meals in the company of others. People living on their own, however, sometimes also get weight problems: either because they cannot be bothered to cook for themselves, so snack off the wrong kinds of food such as jam sandwiches and chocolate biscuits; or because they neglect themselves and do not take enough nourishment.

Elderly ladies, in particular, sometimes quite literally hardly eat enough to keep a bird alive and, in consequence, not only undermine their health but because of their general frailty are more susceptible to falls and broken bones.

A useful leaflet is *Eight Guidelines to a Healthy Diet,* obtainable free from: Food Sense, London SE99 7TP.

Food safety

No discussion about food would be complete without a word on the subject of food safety. As most readers will know, it is inadvisable for anyone to eat uncooked dishes containing raw eggs. To be on the safe side, elderly people should probably also avoid lightly cooked eggs.

When it comes to risk of food poisoning, eggs are by no means the only culprits. 'Cook-chill' foods, including ready-cooked chickens and pork pies, are a breeding ground for bacteria especially in summer. Seafood too can be very dodgy in hot weather.

Storage and cooking play a major part in warding off sickness. The government leaflet *Food Safety* recommends the following basic advice:

- Keep all parts of your kitchen clean
- Aim to keep your refrigerator temperature at a maximum of 5°C
- Keep raw and cooked foods separate and use within the recommended dates
- Cook foods thoroughly
- Do not reheat food more than once and don't keep cooked food longer than two days.

Drink

Most doctors maintain that 'a little bit of what you fancy does you good'. Most healthy adults can enjoy a drink at a party or a glass of wine with dinner without any ill effects and retirement is no reason for giving up these pleasures. Moreover, in small quantities, it can be a very effective nightcap. Where problems begin is when people fancy more than is good for them. Alcoholism is the third great killer after heart disease and cancer.

The condition is far more likely among those who are bored or depressed and who drift into the habit of having a drink to cheer themselves up. The trouble is the habit can become insidious and individuals can quite quickly start becoming dependent on drink. The family doctor will be the first person to check with for medical advice. For those who need moral support, joining AA may be the answer.

Alcoholics Anonymous, PO Box 1, Stonebow House, Stonebow, York YO1 2NJ. T:01904 644026. There are over 3,000 groups around the country. Sufferers assist each other in trying to kick the habit, which is made easier by meeting others with the same problem. Membership is free. See telephone directory.

Smoking

Any age is a good one to give up smoking. The gruesome facts are that smokers are 20 times more likely to contract lung cancer. They are at more serious risk of suffering from heart disease and are more liable to chronic bronchitis as well as various other ailments.

Aids to will-power include: travelling in non-smoking carriages in the train; leaving your cigarettes behind when you go out; and refusing as a personal point of honour to cadge off friends. Working out how much money you would save and promising yourself a reward on the proceeds could help. Thinking about your health in years to come should be an even more convincing argument. Two organisations that offer support are:

Quitline, Victory House, 170 Tottenham Court Road, London W1P 0HA. T:0800 002200. Advice lines are open from 9.30 a.m. to 9 p.m., weekdays.

Smokeline (Scotland only), T:0800 848484. Available noon to midnight, seven days weekly.

Aches, pains and other abnormalities

Age in itself has nothing to do with the vast majority of ailments. However, many people ignore the warning signs when something is wrong, on the basis that this symptom or that is only to be expected as one becomes older. More often than not, treatment when a condition is still in its infancy can either cure it altogether or at least help to delay its advance.

The following should always be investigated by a doctor:

- any pain which lasts more than a few days
- lumps, however small
- dizziness or fainting
- chest pains, shortness of breath or palpitations
- persistent cough or hoarseness
- unusual bleeding from anywhere
- unnatural tiredness or headaches
- frequent indigestion
- unexplained weight loss.

Health insurance

Many people are covered by private health insurance or provident schemes during their working lives. If you wish to continue this benefit, most groups will be glad to welcome you as an individual client.

Even if you have not previously been insured, it is not too late to consider doing so. Firstly, because a number of low-cost schemes for older people have recently been introduced; secondly, because tax relief (at basic rate) is allowable on private health insurance payments for people aged 60 and over. Provided the scheme is a qualifying policy (permanent health insurance plans i.e. those that pay a cash benefit of more than £5 a night do not qualify), the tax relief is given to whoever actually makes the payment: the individual concerned or their grown-up children (or other relative/friend) buying insurance on their behalf.

Terms and conditions vary but all the major groups offer to pay the greatest part of the costs of in-patient accommodation, treatment and medical fees as well as out-patient charges for specialists, X-rays and similar. However, policies do not normally cover GPs' costs. As with all types of insurance, the small print matters, so make sure you understand exactly what you are being offered (likewise any exclusion clauses) before signing.

Organisations that offer private health insurance include:

BCWA Healthcare, James Tudor House, 90 Victoria Street, Bristol BS1 6DF. T:0117 929 5555.

BUPA, BUPA House, 15-19 Bloomsbury Way, London WC1A 2BA. T:0800 600500.

Exeter Friendly Society, Beech Hill House, Walnut Gardens, Exeter, Devon EX4 4DG. T:01392 75361.

Lloyds Bank Healthcover, 205 Brooklands Road, Weybridge, Surrey KT13 0PE. T:01932 821052.

Norwich Union Healthcare Ltd., Chilworth House, Hampshire Corporate Park, Templars Way, Eastleigh, Hants SO5 3RY. T:01703 266533.

PPP healthcare, PPP House, Upperton Road, Eastbourne, East Sussex BN21 1LH. T:0800 335555.

Prime Health Ltd., Wey House, Farnham Road, Guildford, Surrey GU1 4XS. T:01483 440550.

Provincial Insurance Company (contact your local branch – see telephone directory).

Royal Sun Alliance, Parkside, Chart Way, Horsham, Sussex RH12 1XA, T:0800 300800.

Saga Services Ltd., The Saga Building, Middelburg Square, Folkestone, Kent CT20 1AZ. T:01483 553553.

Western Provident Association Ltd., Rivergate House, Blackbrook Park, Taunton, Somerset TA1 2PE. T:01823 623000.

If you would welcome advice in selecting a plan, you might like to contact **The Private Health Partnership.** They will send you a questionnaire and then help you match your key requirements to the most suitable scheme. There is a charge of £10 (plus VAT). For further information, telephone helpline: 01943 851133. Similarly, **Sedgwick Noble Lowndes Healthcare Ltd.** runs a telephone advice line. T:0117 988 7546.

Private patients – without insurance cover

If you are not insured but want to go into hospital as a private patient, there is nothing to stop you doing so provided your doctor is willing and you are able to pay the bills. The choice is between the private wings of NHS hospitals, hospitals run by charitable or non-profit-making organisations and those run for profit by private companies.

Long-term care insurance

An emergency operation is one thing; long-term care because a person can no longer cope unaided, quite another. A number of insurance companies offer policies to help meet the costs of long-term care (e.g. nursing home or home carer). These include: Prime Health, Commercial Union, Eagle Star, PPP healthcare, Clerical Medical, Hambro Assured, Scottish Amicable, Abbey Life and BUPA.

N.B. Most such policies do not come cheap and the criteria for pay-out are normally pretty stringent. It is essential to ensure that you fully understand all the terms and conditions before signing. Best advice is to consult an independent financial adviser (IFA) for help.

Health screening

Prevention is better than cure and most of the provident associations offer a screening service to check general health. This is usually available to members of health insurance schemes and others alike.

National Health Service. The NHS offers several different screening services of particular relevance to those aged 50-plus. Two are specially for women and the others are more general.

All adults who have not been seen by a GP over the last three years can request to have a general check-up. This will include a few simple tests, such as checking your blood pressure, and the opportunity to discuss any health problems that could be worrying you. People over 75 should be offered an annual health check by their GP, which can either be done in their own home or at the practice premises. As well as general health, the check will cover such matters as eyesight, hearing, possible mobility problems, worries that may be causing depression and similar.

The special women's tests are to screen for cancer of the cervix and breast. All women between 20 and 64 years are offered a smear test at least every five years; and all women between 50 and 64 years are invited for screening by breast X-ray every three years. (Women over 64 can request a breast X-ray every three years.)

You should automatically receive invitations for screening if you are registered with a GP. If not, ask your GP for details or enquire at your local health authority.

Hospital cash plans

These schemes provide a cash sum for every night the insured person spends in hospital. Premiums start from £1 a week, giving a payment of about £18 a day. All benefits are tax-free and are available to anyone joining before age 65. About 28 organisations offer such schemes. A full list can be obtained from: **British Health Care Association**, 24a Main Street, Garforth, Leeds LS25 1AA. T:0113 232 0903.

National Health Service

Most readers will need no introduction to the National Health Service. However, there may be one or two scraps of information that you do not know that may come in useful around retirement.

Choosing a GP

If you move to a new area, you will need to find a new doctor. The best way is normally by recommendation; or you can enquire at your local Health Authority (HA), see telephone directory.

All GPs must now have practice leaflets, available at their premises, with details about the service. The information should include: names, addresses, sex, year of qualification and type of qualifications along with essential practice information such as surgery hours, services provided and arrangements for emergencies and night calls.

Having chosen a doctor, you should take your medical card to the receptionist to get your name registered. This is not automatic as, firstly, there is a limit to the number of patients any one doctor can accept. Also, some doctors prefer to meet potential patients before accepting them on their list. If you do not have a medical card, you will need to fill in a simple form.

If you want to change your GP, you go about it in exactly the same way. You do not need to give a reason for wanting to change and you do not need to ask anyone's permission.

Two useful publications to read are: *The NHS Reforms and You*; and *You and Your GP*. Available free from libraries, HAs and doctors' surgeries.

Help with NHS costs

Many people have an automatic right to free NHS prescriptions. These include: both men and women aged 60 and over; recipients of income support, jobseeker's allowance, family credit and in some cases, disability working allowance (i.e. if they had capital of £8,000 or less when DWA was claimed); those suffering from a specified medical condition.

Recipients of any of the Social Security benefits listed above also have a right to: free dental treatment, free sight test, NHS wigs, a voucher towards the cost of glasses and help with fares to hospital.

Even if you do not qualify automatically, you may be entitled to some help on the grounds of low income. To find out, fill in claim form AG1 – obtainable from Benefits Agency offices and many dentists, opticians and GPs – and send it to the address on the form. If eligible, then depending on your income, you will be sent either an AG2 (full help) or AG3 (partial help) certificate.

For further information about help with NHS costs, see leaflet HC 11, obtainable from Benefits Agency offices, post offices, pharmacists and GPs.

People under 60 who require a lot of prescriptions could save money by purchasing 'a season ticket'. This costs £29.30 for four months; or £80.50 for a year. A season ticket will work out cheaper if you are likely to need more than 5 prescription items in four months, or more than 14 items in twelve months. Obtain Form FP 95 (EC 95 in Scotland) from a post office, pharmacy, Benefits Agency office or your Health Authority.

If you are on income support and have a disability, you may be entitled to certain premiums on top of your ordinary income support allowance. There are four rates: £20.95 (single); £29.90 (couple) for the generally disabled; and £37.15 (single and couples where only one is disabled) for the severely disabled; £74.30 if both are severely disabled.

Various Social Security benefits are also available to those with special problems because of illness. These include:

- *Incapacity Benefit*, see Leaflets IB 201 and IB 202
- *Severe Disablement Allowance*, see Leaflet NI 252
- *Attendance Allowance*, see Leaflet DS 702
- *Disability Working Allowance*, see Leaflet DS 703
- *Disability Living Allowance*, see Leaflet DS 704

All the above leaflets are obtainable from any Social Security office.

Going into hospital

Stories abound of people who wait months for an operation because of shortage of beds. But while waiting lists may stretch from here to eternity in one area, hospitals in another area may have spare capacity. Many patients are unaware that they can ask their doctor to refer them to a surgeon anywhere in Britain.

Finding out which hospitals have beds has become very easy. A **Government Health Information Service** has been established in each region which, among other information, can advise you which hospitals have the shortest waiting lists. Ring freephone: 0800 665544.

The **College of Health** operates a similar helpline, open 9 a.m. to 7 p.m., Monday – Thursday; and Friday, 9 a.m. to 5 p.m. T:0181 983 1133.

Before you can become a patient at another hospital, your GP will of course need to agree to your being referred.

Help is sometimes available to assist patients with their **travel costs** to and from hospital. This applies: if you receive income support or family credit; get a war or MOD disablement pension; or if you have to travel an exceptionally long way to get to hospital. Claims for help can also be made on the grounds of low income. See leaflet HC 11 *Are You Entitled to Help with Health Costs?*

If you go into hospital, you will continue to receive your State pension as normal for six weeks. After that, it will be reduced. See leaflet NI 9 *Going Into Hospital?*, obtainable from any Social Security office.

If you have any complaints while in hospital, you should speak to the special officer who is there to deal with complaints; or if the matter is more serious, you should write to the hospital general manager. They may refer your complaint to the Regional Director of Public Health. If you are still unhappy, you can go to the Health Service Ombudsman – see addresses below.

If you are likely to need help on leaving hospital, ask to see the **Hospital Social Worker.**

Complaints

The Patient's Charter gives you the right to have any complaint about NHS services investigated and to receive a full and prompt written reply.

In the first instance, you should speak to someone close to the cause of the problem, e.g. doctor, nurse, receptionist or practice. If you would prefer to speak to someone who was not involved in your care, you can speak to the 'Complaints Manager' at your local NHS Trust or Health Authority instead (for addresses, see telephone directory). In jargon terms, this first stage is known as Local Resolution.

If you are not satisfied with the reply you receive, you can ask the NHS Trust or health authority for an **Independent Review**. The Complaints Manager should tell you whom to contact.

If you are still dissatisfied after the Review, then the Health Service Ombudsman (known formally as the Health Service Commissioner) might be able to help. His job is to investigate complaints of failure or maladministration across the whole range of services provided by, or for, the NHS. He cannot, however, take up legal causes on a patient's behalf. Addresses to write to are:

Health Service Ombudsman for England, Millbank Tower, Millbank, London SW1P 4QP. T:0171 276 2035.

Health Service Ombudsman for Wales, 4th Floor, Pearl Assurance House, Greyfriars Road, Cardiff CF1 3AG. T:01222 394621.

Health Service Ombudsman for Scotland, 28 Thistle Street, Edinburgh EH2 1EN. T:0131 225 7465.

If you have a complaint, you should get on to the matter fairly quickly. Time limits require you to register complaints within six months of the incident or within six months of your realising that you have reason for complaint (providing this is within twelve months of the incident itself). These time limits may be waived if you have a very good reason why you could not complain sooner.

If you need further advice on the complaints procedure, contact the Community Health Council or CAB or ring the Health Information freeline on 0800 665544.

You could also contact the **Patients Association**, 8 Guilford Street, London WC1N 1DT. T:0171 242 3460.

Eyes

It is advisable to have your eyes checked every year or two. You will not have to pay if: you are registered blind or partially sighted; are prescribed complex lenses; are diagnosed as having diabetes or glaucoma; are over 40 and are a close relative of someone with glaucoma; or if you are a patient of the Hospital Eye Service. You also qualify for a free sight test if you or your partner are getting income support, family credit or, in some cases, disability working allowance.

Even if none of these apply but you have a low income, you may be entitled to a voucher towards the cost. Fill in claim form AG1, obtainable from Benefits Agency offices, hospitals and opticians. You should hear within a few weeks. If you qualify for help you will receive a certificate AG2 or AG3. Wait until you hear before having a sight test, as it is difficult to claim the money back afterwards.

The sight test should establish whether or not spectacles are needed. If they are, you will be given a prescription which is valid for two years. You are under no obligation to buy glasses from the optician who tested your eyes but can get them where you like.

If you are on a low income or if you require exceptionally powerful lenses, you are likely to qualify for a voucher to help towards the cost. For further details, see leaflet G 11 *NHS Sight Tests and Vouchers for Glasses*, obtainable from any optician or Benefits Agency office. People who are registered blind are entitled to a special tax allowance of £1,280 a year.

For people with a more serious sight problem, a great deal of practical help, including special equipment, can be obtained by contacting: **The Royal National Institute for the Blind**, 224 Great Portland Street, London W1N 6AA, T:0171 388 1266.

All the main banks will provide statements in Braille at no extra charge. BT has a free directory enquiry service for blind and disabled customers. Call the free Linkline on: 0800 800150.

See also the 'Leisure Activities to Enjoy' chapter about libraries and other facilities.

Feet

Many people forget about their feet until they begin to give trouble. Corns and bunions if neglected can become extremely painful, and ideally everyone, especially women who wear high heels, should have chiropody treatment from early middle age or even younger.

Chiropody is available on the National Health Service without referral from a doctor being necessary but facilities tend to be very over-subscribed, so in many areas it is only the very elderly or those with a real problem who can get appointments.

Private chiropodists are listed in the *Yellow Pages*; or for names of local state registered practitioners, write to: **Society of Chiropodists and Podiatrists**, 53 Welbeck Street, London W1M 7HE, T:0171 486 3381.

Hearing

Many people find their hearing begins to deteriorate as they get older. There are a variety of aids on the market that can make life easier. For example, BT has a range of special equipment from louder bell tones to flashing light systems. For information, dial BT free on 0800 800150. Hearing aids and batteries are free on the NHS.

The following organisations can give a lot of help and advice.

Hearing Concern, 7-11 Armstrong Road, London W3 7JL. T:0181 743 1110 (voice); 0181 742 9151 (Minicom). Administers the Sympathetic Hearing Scheme and has local social clubs throughout the UK. Membership is £10 a year.

Royal National Institute for Deaf People, 19-23 Featherstone Street, London EC1Y 8SL. T:0171 296 8000 (voice); 0171 296 8001 (Minicom). Publishes a comprehensive range of free leaflets and a monthly magazine. Annual subscription is £16.50.

British Deaf Association, 1–3 Worship Street, London EC2A 2AB. T: 0171 588 3520 (voice); 0171 588 3529 (text). Works to protect and advance the interests of deaf people. It provides an advice and advocacy service and its branches organise social activities in most areas.

Teeth

Dentistry is one of the treatments for which you have to pay, unless you have a low income. Charges are based on 80 per cent of the cost up to a maximum of £330. If you are receiving income support or believe you may be entitled to reduced charges because your income is very low, get leaflet D 11 *NHS Dental Treatment* which explains the eligibility conditions (from any NHS dentist or Benefits Agency office).

Personal relationships

Retirement is a bit like getting married again. It involves a new life style, fresh opportunities and inevitably, as with marriage, a few adjustments to make. He will have to get used to no longer going to a regular job. She will have to start thinking about another meal to prepare and may perhaps feel that she will have to reorganise her routine. It may, of course, be the other way round with the wife retiring later and the husband sighing at the prospect of a regular gourmet lunch to produce.

After years of perhaps hardly seeing each other for more than a few hours a week except for weekends, suddenly almost the whole of every day can be spent together. He may feel hurt that she does not appear more delighted. She may feel guilty about wishing to get on with her normal life. Even in the most loving marriages, the first weeks of retirement – for either partner – can produce tensions that neither had anticipated.

Normally with good will and understanding on both sides any difficulties are quickly resolved and an even deeper, more satisfying relationship develops. However, for some couples it does not work out so easily and it may be helpful to seek skilled guidance.

Relate, Herbert Gray College, Little Church Street, Rugby, Warwickshire CV21 3AP. T:01788 573241. Offers a counselling service to people who are experiencing difficulties in their marriage or other personal relationships.

Each counselling session costs about £25. No-one is turned away if they cannot afford to make a contribution. See local telephone directory under 'Relate' or 'Marriage Guidance' or contact the national headquarters above.

The address for Scotland is: **Marriage Counselling Scotland**, 105 Hanover Square, Edinburgh EH2 1DJ. T:0131 225 5006.

A similar service is offered by: **Marriage Care**, Clitherow House, 1 Blythe Mews, Blythe Road, London W14 0NW. T:0171 371 1341; for Scotland, 196 Clyde Street, Glasgow G1 4JY. T:0141 204 1239; for Ireland, **Accord**, All Hallows College, Drumcondra, Dublin 9. T:00 353 1 371151.

Depression

Depression can be first cousin to marriage and other relationship problems. It is fairly common after bereavement, can be caused by worries or may occur after an operation. Sometimes too, as a number of retired people find, it develops as a result of loneliness, boredom or general lack of purpose.

Usually people come out of it of their own accord but if the condition persists a doctor should always be consulted, as depression can create sleeping difficulties and other problems. Another reason for seeing a doctor is that the symptoms may be due to being physically run down, as after 'flu, and all that is needed is a good tonic – or perhaps a holiday.

Sometimes, however, it may be that rather than medicines or the stimulus of a new activity, individuals may feel they need to talk to someone outside the family circle who has a deeper understanding of what they are experiencing.

The Samaritans, 10 The Grove, Slough, Berkshire SL1 1QP. T:0345 909090. The Samaritans are available at any time of the day or night, every single day of the year. They are there to talk or listen for as long as an individual wants. Although most people think of The Samaritans as being a service for those who feel they may be in danger of taking their own life, you do not need to feel positively suicidal to contact them. If you are simply very depressed, they will equally welcome your call. The service is free and completely confidential. For your local branch, see in the telephone directory under 'S'.

Mind (The Mental Health Charity), Granta House, 15-19 Broadway, London E15 4BQ. T:0181 519 2122. Mind is a national charity that aims to help people in mental distress. There are local groups throughout the country as well as day centres, social clubs, advocacy and self-help groups. Mind also publishes a large range of pamphlets and books. For further information, ring the Mind Infoline on: 0181 522 1728 (for London), 0345 660163 (outside London); or contact your local association (see telephone directory).

Some common afflictions

Quite probably you will be one of the lucky ones and the rest of this chapter will be of no further interest to you. It deals with some of the more common afflictions, such as back pain and heart disease. However, if you are unfortunate enough to be affected, or have a member of your family who is, then knowing which organisations can provide support could make all the difference in helping you to cope.

Arthritis and rheumatism

Arthritis Care, 18 Stephenson Way, London NW1 2HD. T:0171 916 1500. Has over 600 branches offering practical support including a visiting service, transport and social activities. Arthritis Care also provides specially adapted holiday centres. Membership is £6 a year.

The Arthritis & Rheumatism Council, Freepost, Chesterfield, Derbyshire S41 7BR. T:01246 558033. Publishes a large number of free booklets on understanding and coping with arthritis. To receive information pack, please send 9" x 6" sae.

Back pain

Four out of five people suffer from back pain at some stage of their lives. While there are many different causes, doctors agree that much of the trouble could be avoided through correct posture, care in lifting heavy articles, a firm mattress and chairs that provide support in the right places.

The Back Shop, 14 New Cavendish Street, London W1M 7LJ. T:0171 935 9120. A shop and mail order business that sells medically approved products that help prevent back trouble or may provide relief for those who suffer. A free catalogue is available on request.

National Back Pain Association, 16 Elmtree Road, Teddington, Middlesex TW11 8ST. T:0181 977 5474. Funds research into the causes and treatment of back pain and publishes a range of free leaflets to help sufferers. Local branches organise talks, exercise classes and social activities. Membership is £15.

Cancer

One of the really excellent trends in recent years is a far greater willingness to talk about cancer. Quite apart from the fact that discussing the subject openly has removed some of the dread, increasingly one hears stories of people who have made a complete recovery. Early diagnosis can make a vital difference.

Anyone with a lump or swelling, however small, should waste no time in having it investigated by a doctor.

There are a number of excellent support groups for cancer sufferers. Rather than list them all, we have only included two as BACUP, as well as its own services, can act as an information service about other local cancer support groups.

BACUP (British Association of Cancer United Patients), 3 Bath Place, Rivington Street, London EC2A 3JR. Freephone: 0800 181199. Offers a free and confidential telephone information service. Calls are answered by a nurse who has the time, knowledge and understanding to answer your questions.

A London and Glasgow based one-to-one counselling service is also available which is free to anyone affected by cancer. BACUP can also put you in contact with local counsellors. Call 0171 696 9000 (London) or 0141 553 1553 (Glasgow). BACUP publishes many booklets on different types of cancer and their treatment. A publications list is available on request.

Breast Cancer Care, Kilm House, 210 New King's Road,

London SW6 4NZ. Freeline: 0500 245345. Offers practical advice and emotional support to women with breast cancer including putting them in touch with others who have had a similar experience. It also offers a prosthesis fitting service.

Diabetes

Diabetes can be diagnosed at any age, although it is common in the elderly and especially among individuals who are overweight.

British Diabetic Association, 10 Queen Anne Street, London W1M 0BD. T:0171 323 1531. Offers an information and advisory service for all diabetics and their families. Over 440 local groups both give support and run social activities; contact Head Office for details. BDA membership costs £15 (£4 for pensioners and people on low income) per year.

Migraine

Migraine affects over 6 million people in Britain. It can involve head pains, nausea, visual disturbance and speech problems.

The Migraine Trust, 45 Great Ormond Street, London WC1N 3HZ. T:0171 831 4818. Offers a service to sufferers including helpline, free information pack and regular newsletters.

Osteoporosis and menopause problems

Osteoporosis, commonly known as the 'brittle bone' disease, kills more women than cancer of the breast, cervix and uterus combined. If often starts around the onset of the menopause when the body begins to lose calcium more rapidly and at least one in three women (and also some men) are affected in some way.

The National Osteoporosis Society, PO Box 10, Radstock, Bath BA3 3YB. T:01761 471771. Offers support and advice on all aspects of osteoporosis. Membership, which is optional, is £10 and entitles you to free newsletters and attendance at annual meetings.

Women's Health Concern (WHC), 93-99 Upper Richmond Road, London SW15 2TG. T:0181 780 3945. WHC offers advice to women with gynaecological and hormonal disturbance problems, in particular with the menopause and proper use of HRT. It runs a telephone counselling service and also sees patients face-to-face at its centres in Peterborough, Newcastle, Surbiton and London. WHC charges no fee but donations are very much appreciated.

Stroke and heart disease

The earlier sections on smoking, diet, drink and exercise list some of the more pertinent, 'dos and don'ts' that can help prevent stroke and heart disease.

The Stroke Association, Stroke House, Whitecross Street, London EC1Y 8JJ. T:0171 490 7999. Provides an advisory service for stroke patients and their families. Home visits can be arranged and more than 500 Stroke clubs offer social and therapeutic support. For information contact the London office above.

Useful publications are also obtainable from the **British Heart Foundation**, 14 Fitzhardinge Street, London W1H 4DH. T:0171 935 0185.

AIDS

If you are concerned about the possibility of Aids and do not feel able to consult your doctor, there are a number of helpful organisations to which you can turn, including:

National Aids Helpline: 0800 567123. Free service, available 24-hours a day.

Terrence Higgins Trust Ltd. Helpline: 0171 242 1010. Hours are 12 noon to 10 p.m. every day.

London Friend. T:0171 837 3337. This is a befriending and counselling agency for 'gay' and bi-sexual men and women. The helpline is open every evening between 7.30 p.m. and 10 p.m. There is a special women's line, on Sunday to Thursday evenings from 7.30 p.m. to 10 p.m., call 0171 837 2782.

GUM Clinics. Genito-urinary-medicine clinics exist in all NHS Hospitals. You can get telephone numbers from your local health authority. Or look in the telephone directory under 'Venereal' or 'Sexually transmitted diseases'.

Disability

Disability is mainly covered in Chapter 11, so if you or someone in your family has a problem, you may find the answer there. In this section, we list some of the key organisations that provide help.

Local authority services

Social Services Departments (Social Work Department in Scotland) provide many of the services which people with disabilities may need, including:

- Practical help in the home, perhaps with the support of a home help
- Adaptations to your home, such as a ramp for a wheelchair or other special equipment
- Meals on wheels
- Provision of day centres, clubs and similar
- Issue of orange badges for cars driven or used by people with a disability (in some authorities this is handled by the Works Department or by the Residents' Parking Department)
- Advice about other transport services or concessions that may be available locally.

A social worker will either make the arrangements or signpost you in the right direction.

Occupational therapists: can advise about special equipment and help teach someone with a disability through training and exercise how best to manage. Contact through the Social Services Department.

Health care

Services are normally arranged either through a GP or the local authority health centre. Key professional staff include:

- Health visitors: qualified nurses who, rather like social workers, will be able to put you in touch with whatever specialised services are required
- District nurses: will visit patients in their home
- Physiotherapists: use exercise and massage to help improve mobility, for example after an operation
- Medical social workers: employed at hospitals and will help with any arrangements before a patient is discharged.

Employment

The Disablement Resettlement Officer helps people looking for work and can also advise about any available grants, for example towards the cost of fares to work. Ask at your nearest Jobcentre.

Equipment

If you have temporary need of, say, a wheelchair, you will normally be able to borrow this from the hospital or local British Red Cross branch. If you want equipment including aids for the home on a more permanent basis, the best source of information is the Disabled Living Foundation Equipment Centre where all sorts of aids can be seen and tried out by visitors. An appointment is essential to enjoy the most benefit from a visit. Contact: **Disabled Living Foundation**, 380 Harrow Road, London W9 2HU, T:0171 289 6111.

If it is not possible for you to come to London, the **Disabled Living Centres Council** (T:0171 820 0567) will be able to recommend a centre nearer your home.

Another very useful organisation to contact for advice on equipment and home adaptations is RADAR – see below.

Finally, BT supplies many aids to enable people with disabilities to use the telephone more easily. For further information, dial BT free on 0800 800150.

Helpful organisations

Fount of all knowledge on almost every topic to do with disability is: **Royal Association for Disability and Rehabilitation (RADAR)**, 12 City Forum, 250 City Road, London EC1V 8AF. T:0171 250 3222.

It can give advice on: statutory and voluntary services, mobility issues, holidays, employment, the National Key Scheme for Toilets for Disabled People (allows disabled people to use public loos when these would normally be locked against vandalism) and much else.

Motability, Customer Information Services, Goodman House, Station Approach, Harlow, Essex CM20 2ET. T:01279 635666. Aims to help recipients of the higher rate mobility component of disability living allowance get value for money when buying or hiring a car or buying a powered wheelchair. They can advise about special discounts and can sometimes give help from their charitable fund.

Other useful addresses include:

Disability Action, 2 Annadale Avenue, Belfast BT7 3JH. T:01232 491011.

Disability Scotland, Princes House, 5 Shandwick Place, Edinburgh EH2 4RG. T:0131 229 8632.

Disability Wales/Anabledd Cymru, Llys Ifor, Crescent Road, Caerphilly CF83 1XL. T:01222 887325.

Health Education Board for Scotland, Woodburn House, Canaan Lane, Edinburgh EH10 4SG. T:0131 536 5500.

Useful reading

Health and Well-Being: A Guide for Older People. Department of Health booklet, obtainable from Department of Health, PO Box 410, Wetherby LS23 7LN.

Disability Rights Handbook. Available from Disability Alliance Educational and Research Association, 1st Floor, Universal House, 88-94 Wentworth Street, London E1 7SA. £10.50 (£6.50 for people in receipt of any means-tested benefit).

Health tips for travellers

If you are going abroad, it is essential to have proper medical insurance. *Which?* recommends cover of: £250,000 for Europe; £1 million for all other parts of the world.

Reciprocal arrangements for emergency treatment exist between Britain and other EC countries but facilities vary greatly both in quality and generosity. A Form E111 is a **must.** See Department of Health leaflet *Health Advice for Travellers* (T5) obtainable from main post offices.

Other advice is plain common sense – but worth repeating for all that.

■ Remember to pack any regular medicines you require: even familiar branded products can be difficult to obtain in some countries.

■ Take a mini first aid kit, including: plaster, disinfectant, tummy pills and so on.

■ If you are going to any under-developed country, consult your doctor as to what pills (and any special precautions) you should take.

■ One of the most common ailments among British travellers abroad is an overdose of sun. In some countries, it really burns, so take it easy, wear a hat and apply plenty of protective lotion.

■ The other big travellers' woe is 'Delhi belly', which unhappily can apply in most hot countries, including Italy and Spain. Beware the water, ice, salads, seafood, ice cream and any fruit which you do not peel yourself. Department of Health advice is only to eat freshly cooked food which is both hot and thoroughly cooked. It is also advisable to check with your doctor.

- Always wash your hands before eating or handling food, particularly if you are camping or caravanning.
- Travelling is tiring and a sudden change of climate more debilitating than most of us admit: allow plenty of time during the first couple of days to acclimatise.
- Have any inoculations or vaccinations well in advance of your departure date.
- When flying, wear loose clothes and above all comfortable shoes as feet and ankles tend to swell in the air. On long journeys, it helps to drink plenty of fruit juice and remember the warning that 'an alcoholic drink in the air is worth two on the ground'. If you have a special diet, inform whoever makes your booking: most airlines, especially on long-distance journeys, serve vegetarian food.
- Finally, the old favourite, don't drink and drive.

Keep fit and have a wonderful holiday!

11

When Parents Need Extra Help

Most of us sooner or later have some responsibility for the care of elderly parents. While there is no hiding the fact that this can impose strains, most families cope exceedingly well.

Knowing what facilities are available, what precautions you can take against a mishap occurring and whom you can turn to in an emergency can make all the difference, both to you and to parents who may fear becoming a burden.

A basic choice for many families is whether parents should move in with them or continue to live on their own. While the decision will depend on individual circumstances, in the early days at least the majority choice is generally in favour of 'staying put'. Although later in the chapter we cover sheltered housing, an alternative solution to any move may be simply to adapt the home to make it safer and more convenient.

Ways of adapting a home

Many even quite elderly people will not require anything more complicated than a few general improvements, such as: better lighting, especially near staircases; a non-slip mat and grab-rail in the bathroom; safe heating arrangements; and perhaps the lowering of some kitchen and other units to place them within easy reach.

Another plan worth considering is to convert a downstairs room into a bedroom and bathroom, in case managing the stairs should later become a difficulty. These and other common-sense measures are discussed in Chapter 7.

For some people, however, such arrangements are not really sufficient. In the case of a physically disabled person, more radical improvements will usually be required. Far from presenting a major problem, today these are normally fairly easy to organise.

Local authority help

Local authorities have a legal duty to help people with disabilities and, depending on what is required and the individual's ability to pay, may assist with the cost.

Your parents can either approach their GP or contact the Social Services department. A doctor will be able to: advise what is needed; supply any prescriptions such as for a medical hoist; and can make a recommendation to the Housing Department, should rehousing be desirable.

The Social Services Department may be able to supply kitchen, bathroom and other aids for the home, arrange an appointment with an occupational therapist and support an application for a housing grant, should major adaptations be required.

Other sources of help

The Disabled Living Foundation, 380-384 Harrow Road, London W9 2HU. T:0171 289 6111. DLF runs an Equipment Centre, staffed by trained therapists, where aids of all kinds for the home can be tried out by visitors. Please phone for an appointment.

The Royal Association for Disability and Rehabilitation (RADAR), 12 City Forum, 250 City Road, London EC1V 8AF. T:0171 250 3222. Can advise on almost all matters to do with disability and the home – plus just about every other topic where disability is an issue.

Both the **British Red Cross** and **Age Concern** (see local telephone directory) may loan equipment in the short term and be able to advise on local stockists.

Keep Able, Fleming Close, Park Farm, Wellingborough, Northants NN8 6UF. A chain of specialist retail stores, stocking a wide range of gadgets to make life easier for disabled and elderly people. For further information, telephone the National Helpline on 0900 202122.

REMAP, Hazeldene, Ightham, Sevenoaks, Kent TN15 9AD. T:01732 883818. Can often help design or adapt goods to suit individuals, where there is no commercially available product to meet their particular needs.

Smith + Nephew Homecraft Ltd., Sidings Road, Low Moor Industrial Estate, Kirkby-in-Ashfield, Notts NG17 7JZ. T:01623 754047. Stocks a wide variety of practical equipment to help older people cope with everyday life. For mail order, telephone Chestercare: 01623 757955.

The Centre for Accessible Environments, Nutmeg House, 60 Gainsford Street, London SE1 2NY. T:0171 357 8182. Runs an architectural advisory service and can recommend local architects with experience of designing for people with disabilities. When writing, you should give broad details of the type of work required.

Other helpful sources of advice include:

Disability Scotland, Princes House, 5 Shandwick Place, Edinburgh EH2 4RG. Tel/Minicom: 0131 229 8632.

Disability Wales/Anabledd Cymru, Llys Ifor, Crescent Road, Caerphilly CF83 1XL. T:01222 887325.

Disability Action, 2 Annadale Avenue, Belfast BT7 3JH. T:01232 491011.

See also Housing Grants and Care and Repair in Chapter 7.

Alarm systems

It is worth thinking about alarm systems. The knowledge that help can be summoned very quickly in the event of an emergency can enable many elderly people to remain independent far longer than would otherwise be sensible. Some local authorities have alarm systems that can link people living in their own homes to a central control. Ask the Social Services Department.

Community alarms. Telephone alarm systems operated on the public telephone network can be used by anyone with a direct telephone line. The systems link into a 24-hour monitoring centre and have a pendant which enables help to be called even when the owner is some distance from the telephone. Grants may sometimes be available. One of the most widely used systems is SeniorLink, run by Help the Aged. For information, ring **SeniorLink Response Centre**, T:01483 773952.

Commercial firms. For advice and a list of suppliers that install and operate alarm systems, contact the Information Service, Disabled Living Foundation, (see page 161).

Main local authority services

Local authorities supply a number of services which can prove invaluable to an elderly person. The two most important are meals on wheels and home helps. Social Services Departments have responsibility for assessing and co-ordinating arrangements for individuals according to their needs.

Meals on wheels

As you will know, the purpose is to deliver a hot lunch to people in their own home. In some areas, the scheme operates seven days a week; in others, only two. Cost also varies: from about 35p to £1.75 a day, with the norm about £1. Contact the Social Services Department or your CAB.

Home helps

Local authorities have a legal obligation to run a home help service to help frail and housebound elderly people with such basic chores as shopping, tidying up, a little light cooking and so on. The service is usually means-tested, so there may be a charge. Apply through the Social Services Department.

Specialist helpers

Local authorities employ a number of specialist helpers who are there to assist.

Social workers. Normally the first people to contact if you have a problem. They can put you in touch with the right person, if you require a home help, meals on wheels, have a housing difficulty or other query and are not sure whom to approach. You should ring the local Social Services Department; in Scotland, this is normally referred to as the Social Work Department.

Occupational therapists. Have a wide knowledge of disability and can assist a disabled person via training, exercise, or access to aids, equipment or adaptations to the home. Ring the Social Services Department.

Health visitors. Qualified nurses with broad knowledge both of health matters and of the various services available via the local authority. Rather like social workers, health visitors can put you in touch with whatever specialised facilities are required. Contact through the local Health Centre.

District nurses. Fully qualified nurses who will visit a patient in the home: change dressings, attend to other routine nursing matters, monitor progress and help with the arrangements if more specialised care is required. Contact through the Health Centre.

Physiotherapists. Use exercise and massage to help improve mobility and strengthen muscles, for example after an operation or to alleviate a crippling condition. Normally available at both hospitals and health centres.

Medical social workers. In the old days, used to be known as almoners. Are available to consult, if patients have any problems – whether practical or emotional – on leaving hospital. MSWs can advise on such matters as transport, after-care and other immediate arrangements. Work in hospitals and an appointment should be made before the patient is discharged.

Key voluntary organisations

Voluntary organisations complement the services provided by statutory health and social services in making life easier for elderly people living at home. The range of provision varies from area to area but can include:

- Lunch clubs
- Aids such as wheelchairs
- Good neighbour schemes
- Holidays and short-term placements
- Odd jobs and decorating
- Prescription collection
- Day centres and clubs
- Transport
- Advice and information
- Friendly visiting
- Gardening
- Family support schemes.

These services are not always provided by the same agency in every area. The CAB will advise you whom to contact. The following are the key agencies:

Age Concern Groups may provide any or all of the services listed above. Most groups recruit volunteers to do practical jobs and provide friendship. See local telephone directory.

Women's Royal Voluntary Service runs some invaluable services:

- Meals on wheels
- Lunch clubs
- Day centres
- Books-on-wheels
- Transport
- Home visiting
- Hospital shops
- Children's holiday schemes

See local phone book or contact the national headquarters: Women's Royal Voluntary Service, Milton Hill House, Milton Hill, Abingdon, Oxon OX13 6AF. T:01235 442900.

British Red Cross also supplies some important services. The principal ones available from many branches include:

- Providing home-from-hospital support
- Escorting sick, disabled or frail people when travelling
- Loaning equipment short-term for sick or convalescent patients at home, e.g. wheelchairs and commodes
- After-care and home visiting (including practical help in such tasks as hair washing, shopping, changing library books)
- Sitting-in with elderly people and those with disabilities
- Providing transport for the housebound
- Christmas shopping
- 'Signposting' sick people and those with disabilities towards the statutory or voluntary services from which their needs may best be met.

To contact your local British Red Cross branch, see telephone directory, or write to: **British Red Cross (BRCS)**, 9 Grosvenor Crescent, London SW1X 7EJ. T:0171 235 5454.

St. John Ambulance volunteers help in hospitals and sometimes also assist people at home with, say, the shopping or by providing transport to and from hospital. In some areas loan of equipment such as wheelchairs can be arranged. To get in touch, see local telephone directory or contact: **St. John Ambulance**, 1 Grosvenor Crescent, London SW1X 7EF. T:0171 235 5231.

Other sources of help and advice

Civil Service Retirement Fellowship, 1b Deals Gateway, Blackheath Road, London SE10 8BW. T:0181 691 7411. Runs a home visiting service and organises a wide range of social activities for retired civil servants and their families through its many branches.

Counsel & Care, Twyman House, 16 Bonny Street, London NW1 9PG. T:0171 485 1566 (10.30 a.m. – 4 p.m.). Provides a free confidential advisory service, which is used by thousands of elderly people and their relatives each year.

Central Council for Jewish Community Services, 17 Highfield Road, London NW11 9LS. T:0181 458 1035. CCJCS is an umbrella organisation for Jewish community services with over 60 affiliated member organisations. It publishes a *Directory of Jewish Social Services*, listing facilities throughout the UK.

Services for elderly Jewish people in London and the South East are run by **Jewish Care**, 221 Golders Green Road, London NW11 9DQ. Main facilities include: kosher meals service, day centres plus some residential homes. Outside London, contact:

Leeds Jewish Welfare Board, 311 Stonegate Road, Leeds LS17 6AZ. T:0113 268 4211.

Manchester Jewish Community Care, Nicky Alliance Day Centre, 85 Middleton Road, Crumpsall, Manchester M8 4JY. T:0161 740 0111.

Brighton & Hove Jewish Welfare Board, 76 Marmion Road, Hove, East Sussex BN3 5FT. T:01273 722523.

Merseyside Jewish Welfare Council, Shifrin House, 433 Smithdown Road, Liverpool 15. T:0151 733 2292.

SSAFA Forces Help (formerly SSAFA and the Forces Help Society), 19 Queen Elizabeth Street, London SE1 2LP. T:0171 403 8783. Provides whatever help may be needed to retired people who have served in HM Forces. This may typically include advice on pensions and benefits or the provision of a grant for a special need.

Transport

The difficulty of getting around is often a major problem for elderly people. The Department of Transport produces the following useful database of services and is also responsible for running MAVIS.

Voluntary and Community Schemes Database. Lists details of hundreds of transport schemes around the country helpful to elderly and/or disabled people, including those needing to use a wheelchair. For further information, T:0171 271 5252 (voice and minicom).

Mobility Advice and Vehicle Information Service (MAVIS), O'wing Macadam Drive, Old Wokingham Road, Crowthorne, Berkshire RG45 6XD. T:01344 661000. MAVIS is an information service advising on all aspects of mobility – in particular, problems associated with driving. Its services include assessment of elderly motorists wishing to return to driving after a stroke or other disabling illness and advice on low-cost adaptations to relieve the pain of arthritic joints or other conditions that make driving uncomfortable. While general information is free, there is a charge for the more specialised services.

See also 'Disability Living Allowance', page 171.

Driving licence renewal at age 70

All drivers aged 70 are sent a licence renewal form and have to pay a £6 fee to have their licence renewed. The licence has to be renewed (and £6 paid) at least every three years. Depending on their health and eyesight, the driver might be sent a new form after only one or two years. If this applies, the form must be completed honestly but no extra charge will be made.

Temporary living-in help and flexi-care

Elderly people living alone can be more vulnerable to 'flu and other winter ailments. They may have a fall or, for no apparent reason, go through a period of being forgetful and neglecting themselves. In the event of an emergency, living-in help can be a godsend. Most agencies tend inevitably to be on the expensive side, although in a crisis often represent excellent value for money. Another longer-term possibility is to recruit a Community Service Volunteer.

Community Service Volunteers, 237 Pentonville Road, London N1 9NJ. T:0171 278 6601. Match full-time helpers with people who need a high degree of support. The volunteers, ages 16 to 35, are untrained and work for periods of 4 to 12 months. They provide companionship and practical assistance in the home.

Schemes are usually set up through a social worker, who supervises how the arrangement is working. There is an annual retainer of £1,848 (in case of real financial need, the local authority might pay) plus other expenses of about £50 a week. Contact the Social Services Department; or approach CSV direct.

Agencies. Both weekly charges and booking fees vary. Payment is normally gross, so your parents will not be involved in having to work out tax or national insurance. For a list of agencies, see *Yellow Pages* under heading 'Domestic' or 'Domestic Staff'.

A problem for many elderly people is that the amount of care they need is liable to vary according to their health and other factors including, for example, the availability of neighbours and family. Whereas after an operation the requirement may be for someone with basic nursing skills, a few weeks later the only need may be for someone to act as a companion – or simply to pop in for the odd hour during the day. An organisation well worth knowing about is:

United Kingdom Home Care Association, 42 Banstead Road, Carshalton Beeches, Surrey SM5 3NW. T:0181 288 1551. It represents over 1,000 agencies that specialise in providing care for older people. All requirements are catered for, including temporary and permanent posts, residential, daily, overnight and hourly work.

Nursing care

If one of your parents needs regular nursing care, their doctor may be able to arrange for a district nurse to visit them at home. This will not be a sleeping-in arrangement – simply a qualified nurse calling round when necessary.

If you want more concentrated home nursing you will have to go through a private agency. Many arrange hourly, daily or live-in nurses on a temporary or longer term basis. One of the best known, with over 130 branches throughout the UK, is **BNA**, The Colonnades, Beaconsfield Close, Hatfield, Herts AL10 8YD. T:01707 263544. (See telephone directory for branch addresses.)

Emergency care for pets

For many elderly people a pet is a most important part of their lives, providing companionship and fun as well as stimulating them into taking regular outdoor exercise. But in the event of the owner having to go into hospital or due to some other emergency being temporarily unable to care for their pet, there can be real problems including concern for the welfare of the animal and considerable distress to the owner.

To overcome these problems, two imaginative schemes have been set up, one operating throughout the UK and the other just in Scotland. Depending on what is required, volunteers will either simply feed or exercise the animal or will care for it in their own home until the owner can manage again.

Cinnamon Trust, Foundry House, Foundry Square, Hayle, Cornwall TR27 4HH. T:01736 757900. As well as the above services, Cinnamon also arranges permanent care for pets whose owners have died. Emergency services can be called 24 hours a day. The Trust makes no charge but donations, or a bequest, are very much appreciated.

Pet Fostering Service Scotland. T:01877 331496. The only charges are the cost of pet's food, litter – in the case of cats – and any veterinary fees that may be necessary.

Practical help for carers

If your parent is still fairly active the difficulties may be fairly minimal. However, in the case of an ill or very frail person far more intensive care may be required.

If you go out to work, have other responsibilities or quite understandably feel that if you are to remain human you must have time for your own interests, it is important to know what help is available and how to obtain it.

The many services provided by local authorities and voluntary agencies, described earlier in the chapter, apply for the most part equally to an elderly person living with their family as to one living alone. If none of these solves your problems, ask your CAB or Social Services Department, as there may be some special local facility that could provide the solution.

In particular, you might ask about **day centres and clubs**. A responsible person will always be in charge and transport, to and from the venue, is often provided. Most areas also have **respite care facilities** to enable carers to take a break. This could be for just the odd day or longer, to allow carers who need it to have a real rest. Contact your Health or Social Services department.

Another service worth knowing about is **Crossroads**. It arranges for attendants to care for very frail or disabled people in their own home, while the regular carer is away. They will come in during the day, or stay overnight, as necessary. There is no charge but donations are welcomed. Priority is given to those in greatest need. Ask at the CAB or contact: **Crossroads**, Caring for Carers, 10 Regent Place, Rugby, Warwickshire CV21 2PN. T:01788 573653.

Holidays

There are various schemes to enable families with a dependent relative to go on holiday alone or simply to enjoy a respite from their caring responsibilities.

Some local authorities run **fostering schemes,** on similar lines to child fostering. Elderly people are invited to stay with a neighbour and live in the household as an ordinary family member. There may be a charge or the service may be run on a voluntary basis. Ask Social Services.

Some charities organise **holidays for older people** to give relatives a break. The Volunteer Bureau or Social Services should have details.

Another solution is a **short-stay home,** which is residential accommodation variously run by local authorities, voluntary agencies or private individuals. Again, Social Services should be able to advise.

If proper medical attention is necessary, consult your parent's GP. **Many hospitals and nursing homes** offer short-stay care as a means of relieving relatives and a doctor should be able to help organise this for you.

Fount of almost all knowledge on anything to do with caring is: **Carers National Association,** 20-25 Glasshouse Yard, London EC1A 4JS. T:0171 490 8818. It has branches throughout the UK and there is a bi-monthly magazine. Annual membership is £5.

Useful reading
Caring for Someone?, free from Social Security offices.

Benefits and allowances

There are a number of benefits/allowances available to those with responsibility for the care of an elderly person and/or to elderly people themselves.

Entitlements for carers

Home responsibilities protection. A means of protecting your State pension if you are unable to work because of the need to care for an elderly person. See 'Understanding Your Pension' chapter (page 47) or ask any Social Security office for form CF 411.

Invalid care allowance. People under 65 who do not work full-time because they have to care for a severely disabled person (i.e. someone who gets Attendance Allowance, Constant Attendance Allowance or the two higher care components of Disability Living Allowance) may qualify to receive ICA. You do not need to live at the same address. The basic allowance is £37.35 a week (1997/98) and counts as taxable income. For further details and a claim form, get pack DS 700 from your local Benefits Agency.

Entitlements for elderly/disabled people

More generous income tax allowances. Both the personal allowance and the married couple's allowance are increased when an individual becomes 65; and are raised again after their 75th birthday. Details of the increases, and how these are calculated, are explained in the 'Tax' chapter, pages 51–30.

Attendance Allowance. This is paid to severely disabled people of 65 and over who have needed almost constant care for at least six months. Those who are terminally ill can receive the allowance without having to wait.

There are two different rates: £49.50 a week for those needing 24-hour care; and £33.10 for those needing intensive day or night care. The allowance is tax free and is paid regardless of income (although special rules may apply to people entering residential care). For further details and a claim form, get leaflet DS 702 from any Social Security office.

Disability Living Allowance (DLA). This benefit is paid to people up to the age of 65 inclusive who become disabled. It has two components – a mobility component and a care component. A person can be entitled to either one or to both components.

There are two rates for the mobility part of the allowance and three rates for the care component. More severely disabled people receive the higher amounts.

The (1997/98) rates for the mobility element are £34.60 and £13.15 a week.

The three rates for the care element are: £49.50; £33.10; and £13.15.

DLA is tax free and is paid regardless of income (although special rules may apply to people entering residential care).

For further information get leaflet DS 704, from any post office, CAB or Social Security office.

Cold Weather Payments. These are designed to give particularly vulnerable people extra help with heating costs during very cold weather. Anyone aged 60 and over who gets income support qualifies automatically. The amount paid (at time of writing) is £8.50 a week and those eligible should receive it without having to claim. In the event of a problem, contact your local DSS office.

Financial assistance

A number of charities give financial assistance to elderly people in need. Most have particular criteria such as, for example, a service background, disability, religion or other. To find out which would be worth approaching, ask your library for: *A Guide to Grants for Individuals in Need*, published by the Directory of Social Change;

also *The Charities Digest*, published by the Family Welfare Association.

Special accommodation

Retired people who need particular support may choose or need to move to accommodation where special services are provided. This can either be sheltered housing or a residential home. Both terms cover an enormous spectrum, so anyone considering either of these options should make a point of investigating thoroughly before reaching a decision.

Sheltered housing

Sheltered housing is usually a development of purpose-designed bungalows or flats within easy access of shops and public transport. They generally have a warden, an alarm system and some common facilities, such as: a garden, launderette and a dining room where meals are provided, on an optional basis, either once a day or several days a week.

Sheltered housing is available for sale or rental, variously through private developers, housing associations or local authorities.

Sheltered housing for sale

Flats and houses are normally sold on long leases (99 years or more). Should a resident decide to move, the property can usually be sold on the open market, provided the prospective buyer is over 55 years of age. Most developers impose a levy of 1 per cent of the sale price for checking the credentials of incoming residents. Look carefully at any schemes that enable you to buy the property at a discount as some entitle the developer to retain part of the equity on resale.

There will be a weekly or monthly service charge and residents normally have to enter into a management agreement with the housebuilder. It is important to be sure exactly what the commitment is before buying. Factors to check include: who the managing agent is; the warden's duties; what the service charge covers; the ground rent; the arrangements for any repairs that might be necessary; whether there is a residents' association; whether pets are allowed; what the conditions are with regard to reselling the property – and the tenant's rights in the matter.

Prices range from approximately £45,000 to £250,000 – depending on size, location and type of property. Weekly service charges vary between roughly £18 and £30, with £22–£27 being the norm.

The service charge usually covers: the cost of the warden, alarm system, maintenance, repair and renewal of any communal facilities (external and internal) and sometimes the heating and lighting costs. It may also cover insurance on the building (but not the contents). Be wary of service charges that seem uncommonly reasonable, as these are often increased well above inflation following purchase.

Those on lowish incomes may be able to get housing benefit to meet some or all of the service charge. For advice, ask at the Housing Department.

The following organisations can provide information about sheltered housing for sale:

Sheltered Housing Services, 8-9 Abbey Parade, North Circular Road, London W5 1EE. T:0181 997 9313. Can advise about most current sites and resales countrywide. Cost of enquiry, plus up-dating service for a year, is £7.50.

AIMS (formerly SHACS), Walkden House, 3-10 Melton Street, London NW1 2EJ. T:0171 383 2006. Offers guidance on points to check before signing any purchase agreement. Will also help anyone with problems living in private sector sheltered housing.

Rented sheltered housing

This is normally provided by local authorities, housing associations and certain benevolent societies. As with accommodation to buy, quality varies.

Local authorities. This is usually only available to local residents. There is often a minimum/maximum age and applicants may be asked to have a medical examination. Apply to the local Housing or Social Services Department.

Housing associations. Supply much of the newly built sheltered housing. Rents, which sometimes include service charge, vary very roughly from £40 to £75 a week.

Some charitable housing associations offer a licensee arrangement which does not provide the same security of tenure as other tenancy agreements. You are strongly advised to have the proposed contract checked by a lawyer before signing it.

CABs and Housing Departments often keep a list of local

housing associations. Otherwise contact: **Housing Corporation,** 149 Tottenham Court Road, London W1P 0BN. T:0171 393 2000.

For Scotland, Wales and Northern Ireland, contact:

Housing for Wales/Tai Cymru, 25-30 Lambourne Crescent, Llanishen, Cardiff CF4 5ZJ. T:01222 741500.

Scottish Homes, Thistle House, 91 Haymarket Terrace, Edinburgh EH12 5HE. T:0131 313 0044.

Northern Ireland Federation of Housing Associations, Carlisle Memorial Centre, 88 Clifton Street, Belfast BT13 1AB. T:01232 230446.

Benevolent societies. These all cater for specific professional and other groups, for example: SSAFA Forces Help and Teachers' Benevolent Fund.

Almshouses

This is sheltered housing for elderly people of reduced means, which is administered by a charitable trust. Rents are not charged but there may be a maintenance contribution towards upkeep and heating. For further information, write to: **The Almshouse Association,** Billingbear Lodge, Wokingham, Berkshire RG40 5RU. T:01344 452922.

Community care

Anyone needing help in arranging suitable care for an elderly person should contact their local Social Services department. They will assess what type of provision would best meet the needs of the individual. This could be either services or special equipment to enable them to stay in their own home; residential home accommodation; or a nursing home. If residential or nursing home care is necessary, the department will arrange a place, pay the charge and seek reimbursement according to the person's means. (See 'Financial Assistance for Residential and Nursing Home Care', page 175).

Residential care homes

The accommodation usually consists of a bedroom plus communal dining rooms, lounges and gardens. All meals are provided, rooms are cleaned and staff are at hand to give whatever help is needed. Most homes are fully furnished, though it is usually possible to take small items of furniture. Except in some of the more expensive private homes, bathrooms are normally shared.

Homes are run by private individuals (or companies), voluntary organisations and local authorities. All private and voluntary homes should be registered with the Social Services to ensure minimum standards. No home should ever be accepted 'on spec'. It is very important that the person should have a proper chance to visit it and ask any questions.

Private homes. Private rest homes tend to be smaller than those run by councils, taking up to about 30 people. Fees cover an enormous range, starting from about £250 a week – and from about £300 in London.

Voluntary rest homes. These are run by charities, religious bodies or other voluntary organisations. Eligibility may be determined by age, background, occupation or general fitness. Fees range from about £208 to £400 a week – higher for Greater London.

Local authority homes. These are sometimes referred to as 'Part III Accommodation' and admission would invariably be arranged by Social Services. If someone does not like the particular accommodation suggested, they can turn it down and ask the department what other offers might be available. Weekly charges start from about £208. However, see Financial Assistance, below.

Nursing homes

Nursing homes provide medical supervision and fully qualified nurses, 24 hours a day. Most are privately run, with the remainder supported by voluntary organisations. All nursing homes must be registered with the local Health Authority which keeps a list of what homes are available in the area.

Private. Average fees are between £335 and £500 a week; with some of the plusher nursing homes very much more expensive. For information contact: **The Registered Nursing Home Association,** Calthorpe House, Hagley Road, Edgbaston, Birmingham B16 8QY. T:0121 454 2511.

Voluntary organisations. Charges start around £300 – £325 a week. Applications should be made either via Social Services or direct to the home manager.

Financial assistance for residential and nursing home care

Under the community care arrangements people needing to go into a residential or nursing home may receive help from their Social Services department.

As explained earlier, the department will make the arrangements direct with the home following their assessment procedure and will seek reimbursement from the person towards the cost, according to set means-testing rules.

People who were already in a residential or nursing home before April 1993 continue receiving special levels of income support as before. The current maximum weekly amount (1997/98) for residential care homes is between £208 and £285 (£41 higher in London); and for nursing homes, between £312 and £352 (£46 higher in London).

People who had been or are currently paying for themselves but can no longer afford to do so may have the right to claim help, now or in the future, if they qualify on grounds of financial need – for example if their savings fall to £16,000. People with assets below £10,000 will not have to pay anything.

Further information

Key sources of information about voluntary and private homes are: the *Charities Digest* and the *Directory of Independent Hospitals and Health Services*. Ask at the library.

Elderly Accommodation Counsel, 46a Chiswick High Road, London W4 1SZ. T:0181 742 1182. Has a nationwide register of 'care' accommodation including sheltered housing, residential care and nursing homes. Listings supplied are tailored to individual requirements re location, care needs and price range.

Grace Consulting, 35 Walnut Tree Close, Guildford, Surrey GU1 4UL. T:0800 137669. Provides an advisory service for those seeking the best options for residential or nursing home care or alternatively for care in their own home. Fees, charged according to the amount of work, start at £50 plus VAT.

Help the Hospices, 34-44 Britannia Street, London WC1X 9JG. T:0171 278 5668. Umbrella organisation for Hospices and Day Care Centres nationwide. Can provide list of independent hospices and other information.

Cinnamon Trust, Foundry House, Foundry Square, Hayle, Cornwall TR27 4HH. T:01736 757900. Maintains a register of residential and care homes that allow pets to be kept.

Some special problems

A minority of people, as they become older, suffer from special problems which can cause great distress. Because families do not like to talk about them, they may be unaware of what services are available so may be missing out both on practical help and sometimes also on financial assistance.

Hypothermia

Elderly people tend to be more vulnerable to the cold. If the body drops below a certain temperature, it can be dangerous because one of the symptoms of hypothermia is that sufferers no longer actually feel cold. For this reason, during a cold snap it is very important to check up regularly on an elderly person living alone.

The **Winter Warmth Line** is a freephone advice service, run by Help the Aged. As well as give practical information, it can refer you to a local help agency. Dial: 0800 289404.

Insulation can play a large part in keeping a home warmer and cheaper to heat. There are various grants available to assist with this. See heating and insulation sections in Chapter 7.

Your parents might qualify for cold weather payments. See page 171.

Incontinence

Incontinence can cause deep embarrassment to sufferers as well as inconvenience to relatives. A doctor should always be consulted, as it can often be cured or at least alleviated by proper treatment. Some local authorities operate a laundry service which collects soiled linen, sometimes several times a week. The person to talk to is the Health Visitor or District Nurse (ring the Health Centre) who will be able to advise about this and other facilities.

InconTact (National Association on Incontinence) offers information and support to people whose lives are affected by bladder and bowel problems. An Incontinence Information Helpline, staffed by nurses with a special understanding of these conditions, operates Monday to Friday from 9 a.m. to 6 p.m. T:0191 213 0050.

Dementia

Sometimes an elderly person can become confused, forgetful or have violent mood swings and at times be abnormally aggressive. It is important to consult a doctor as soon as possible as the cause may be due to depression, stress or even vitamin deficiency, all of which can be treated and often completely cured.

If dementia is diagnosed, it is usually a good idea to talk to the Health Visitor, as she will know about local support services and can also arrange appointments with other professionals.

Two organisations that can often give help and support are:

Alzheimer's Disease Society, Gordon House, 10 Greencoat Place, London SW1P 1PH. T0171 306 0606.

Mind (The Mental Health Charity), Granta House, 15-19 Broadway, London E15 4BQ. T:0181 519 2122.

12

Wills, Benefits and Helpful Organisations

In Bali death is celebrated with glorious processions, merry-making and days of feasting. In Western society, we go to the other extreme. Many people never even get round to making a will, let alone discussing with their partner the financial and other practicalities should one of them die. Yet, as every widows' organisation would testify, a great deal of heartbreak and real financial worry could be avoided if husbands and wives were more open with each other.

Wills

Anyone who is married or over the age of 35 should make a will. At the very least, this will ensure that their wishes are known and properly executed. It will also spare their family the legal complications that arise when someone dies intestate. A major problem if someone dies without leaving a will is that their partner will usually have to wait very much longer for badly needed cash. There will be no executor. Also, the individual's assets will be distributed according to a rigid formula, which may be a far cry from what he or she had intended.

Making a will

You have three choices: you can do it yourself; you can ask your bank to help you; or you can use a solicitor.

Doing it yourself
Homemade wills are not generally recommended. People often use imprecise wording, which could result in the donor's wishes being misinterpreted and could also cause delay in settling the estate.

You can buy forms from W H Smith and other stationers which, while helpful, still leave considerable margin for error.

Two witnesses are needed and an essential point to remember is that beneficiaries cannot witness a will; nor can the spouses of any beneficiaries. In certain circumstances, a will can be rendered invalid. A sensible precaution for anyone doing it themselves is to have it checked by a solicitor or by a legal expert from the CAB.

Banks

Advice on wills and the administration of estates is carried out by the trustee companies of most of the major high street banks.

The services they offer are: to provide general guidance, to act as executor and to administer the estate. They will also introduce clients to a solicitor and keep a copy of the will – plus other important documents – in their safe, to avoid the risk of their being mislaid. Additionally, banks (as solicitors) can give inheritance tax planning and other financial advice. Some banks will draw up a will for you.

Solicitors

Solicitors may offer to: draw up a will, act as executors and administer the estate and keep a copy of your will in safe keeping. If you do not know a solicitor, you can ask the Citizens Advice Bureau or you can look in the *Solicitors Regional Directory* at your library.

Charges

These can vary enormously, depending on the size and complexity of the will. A basic will could be as little as £50 or, if your affairs are more complicated, the cost could run into many hundreds of pounds. Always ask for an estimate before proceeding. Remember too that professional fees carry 17.5 per cent VAT.

Solicitors charge according to the time they spend on a job, so although the actual work may not take very long, if you spend hours discussing your will, or changing it every few months, the costs can escalate very considerably.

Legal aid

Legal aid is available to certain groups of people for making a will. These include: people aged over 70, people with a mental disorder and those who are blind, deaf or have no speech. To qualify, they will need to satisfy the financial criteria. For further information enquire at your CAB.

Executors

You will need to appoint at least one executor. He/she can be a beneficiary under the estate, and can be a member of your family or a friend. Or, and this is generally advisable for larger estates, you could appoint your solicitor or bank.

The fees will be additional. They are not paid at the time of making the will but instead come out of the estate. Significant sums could be involved, so the advice on obtaining an estimate is, if anything, even more relevant. In certain instances, banks can be more expensive; in others, solicitors. The only way to discover is to get an estimate from each.

Banks publish a tariff of their charges. Solicitors render bills according to the time involved; so, although it is impossible for them to be precise, they should nevertheless be able to give a reasonable estimate – at least at the time of quoting. Both banks' and solicitors' fees may increase during the interval between their being appointed and fulfilling their duties as executor.

Other Points

Wills should always be kept in a safe place – and their whereabouts known.

You might find it helpful to obtain a mini-form, known as a Personal Assets Log, to give to your executor or close relatives. It is, quite simply, a four-sided leaflet with space to record the essential information: name and address of solicitor; where the will and other important documents are kept; the date of any codicils and so on. Logs should be obtainable from most solicitors.

Wills may sometimes need updating. For example: an existing will becomes invalid in the event of marriage or remarriage and should be revised. Any changes must be by codicil (for minor alterations) or by a new will, and must be properly witnessed.

If you have views about your funeral, it is sensible to write a letter to your executors explaining your wishes and to lodge it with your will. If you have any pets, you may equally wish to leave a letter filed with your will explaining what arrangements you have made for their immediate/long term welfare. The charity PRO Dogs provides special cards for this purpose for owners to complete, obtainable from: **PRO Dogs**, National Head Office, Rocky Bank, 4 New Road, Ditton, Maidstone, Kent ME20 6AD. T.01732 848499.

Money worries – and how to minimise them

Most people say that the first time they really think about death, in terms of what would happen to their family, is after the birth of their first baby. As children grow up, requirements change but key points that any family man or woman should consider are life insurance and mortgage protection relief.

Both husbands and wives should have **life insurance cover**. If either were to die, not only would their partner lose the benefit of their earnings, they would also lose the value of their services: home decorating, gardening, cooking and so forth.

Most banks and building societies urge homeowners to take out **mortgage protection schemes.** If you die, the loan is paid off automatically and the family home will not be repossessed. Banks also offer **insurance to cover any personal or other loans.** This could be a vital safeguard to avoid leaving the family with debts.

Many people worry about **funeral costs.** These can vary, in different parts of the country, from about £875 to £1,500 or even more depending on the choice of coffin and other arrangements. Although you may hear of cheaper estimates, these are normally exclusive of disbursements which have to be made to the vicar and others.

As a way of helping, some insurance companies offer savings plans to cover funeral costs and while these could be sensible, a drawback is that you are budgeting today against an unknown cost in the future.

A rather different type of scheme which overcomes the uncertainties is the pre-paid funeral plan, whereby you pay all the costs in advance, so sparing your family the worry of finding the money at the time.

One such scheme is the Guaranteed Funeral Plan offered by **Chosen Heritage.** T:0800 525 555. Another is **Perfect Assurance,** which is a 'bespoke' policy tailored to individual requirements, offered by: **National Association of Funeral Directors,** 618 Warwick Road, Solihull, West Midlands B91 1AA. T:0121 709 0019.

While most pre-payment schemes are problem-free, there can be pitfalls – including the risk of losing your money, if the company which sold you the plan ceased trading. Advice from the OFT is to check the following points before paying: (1) whether your money will be paid into a trust administered by independent trustees (2) what fees are deducted from the investment (3) what exact expenses the plan covers.

People on low incomes may qualify for a payment from the Social Fund to help with funeral costs. For details see leaflet D 49, *What To Do After A Death*, obtainable from any Social Security office. If the matter is urgent, make a point of asking for Form SF 200.

A very real crisis for some families is the need for immediate money while waiting for the estate to be settled. At least part of the problem can be overcome by couples having a **joint bank account,** with both partners having drawing rights without the signature of the other being required. Sole-name bank accounts and joint accounts requiring both signatures are frozen.

For the same reason, it may also be a good idea for any savings or investments to be held in the joint name of the couple.

An essential practical point for all couples is that any financial and **other important documents should be discussed together.** Even today, an all too common saga is for widows to come across insurance policies and other papers, which they have never seen before and do not understand – often causing quite unnecessary anxiety. A further common-sense 'must' is for both partners to **know where important papers are kept.** Best idea is either to lock them, filed together, in a home safe; or to give them to the bank for safe keeping.

If someone dies, **the bank manager should be notified as soon as possible,** so he can assist with the problems of unpaid bills and help work out a solution until the estate is settled. The same goes for the **suppliers of essential services:** gas, electricity, telephone and so on. Unless they know the situation, there is a risk of services being cut off if there is a delay in paying the bill. Add too any credit card companies, where if bills lie neglected, the additional interest could mount up alarmingly.

Useful reading

What To Do When Someone Dies, £9.99. Available from Which? Ltd., Castlemead, Gascoyne Way, Hertford X, SG14 1LH.
What To Do After A Death. Free booklet from Social Security offices.
Making Your Will and *Arranging A Funeral*, free factsheets from Age Concern England or Age Concern Scotland (enclose sae).

State benefits, tax and other money points

Some extra financial benefits are given to widows and, in more limited circumstances, to widowers. Several take the form of a cash payment. Others come in the form of a relief against tax.

Benefits paid in cash form

There are three important cash benefits to which widows may be entitled: widows' payment, widows' pension and widowed mother's allowance. To claim these, fill in Form BW 1, obtainable from any Social Security office. You will also be given a questionnaire (BD 8) by the Registrar. It is important that you complete this as it acts as a trigger to speed up payment of your benefits. All leaflets quoted are obtainable from any Social Security office.

Widows' payment. This is a tax free lump sum of £1,000, paid as soon as a woman is widowed provided that: (1) her husband had paid sufficient NI contributions (2) she is under 60; or (3) if she is over 60, her husband had not been entitled to retirement pension. Her claim will not be affected if she is already receiving a State pension, based on her own contributions. See leaflet NP 45 *A Guide to Widows' Benefits*.

Widowed mother's allowance. This is paid to mothers with at least one child for whom they receive child benefit. The value is £62.45 a week. The allowance is usually paid automatically. If, although eligible, you do not receive it, inform your Social Security office. See leaflet NP 45.

Child dependency addition. This is a payment of £11.20 a week for each dependent child except the eldest, for whom payment is £9.90. See leaflet NP 45.

Widows' pension. There are various levels of widows' pension: the full rate which is described immediately below, and age-related widows' pension, which is described in the following paragraph.

Full-rate widows' pension is paid to widows who are aged between 55 and 59 when their husband dies; or when they cease to receive widowed mother's allowance. The current weekly amount is £62.45. It is normally paid once you have sent off your completed form BW 1; so if for any reason you do not receive the pension after about three weeks, you should enquire at your Social Security office.

Age-related widows' pension. This is a pension for younger widows, aged between 45 and 54 inclusive when their husband dies; or when their widowed mother's allowance ceases to be paid. Rates depend on age and vary from £18.74 for 45-year-olds to £58.08 for those aged 54.

Retirement pension. Once a widow reaches 60, she can choose whether to continue with her widows' pension or receive retirement pension instead. After her 65th birthday, she no longer has a choice and will get retirement pension. If she is over 60 when her husband dies, she will also usually receive a retirement pension. If at the time of death the couple were already getting the State retirement pension, the widow will be entitled to her husband's share of their joint pension, if this is higher than her own.

N.B. A widow may be able to use her late husband's NI contributions to boost the amount she receives. See leaflets NP 46 *A Guide to Retirement Pensions* and FB 6 *Retiring? Your Pension and Other Benefits.*

Problems. Pension payments – including widows' pension – are dependent on sufficient NI contributions having been paid. Your Social Security office will inform you if you are not eligible. If this should turn out to be the case, you may still be entitled to receive some other benefit or money from the Social Fund – so ask. If you are unsure of your position or have difficulties, ask at your Citizens' Advice Bureau who will be able to help you work out the sums and inform you of your rights.

Particular points to note

■ Most widows' benefits are taxable. However, the £1,000 lump sum widow's payment is tax free, as are war widows' pensions and the child dependency allowance.

■ There is no widowers' pension. A widower getting a retirement pension at less than the full rate may be able to use his late wife's contributions to get extra.

■ A widower with dependent children will receive child benefit.

■ Men and women widowed after April 1979 will normally inherit their spouse's additional pension rights, if he/she contributed to SERPS; or at least half their guaranteed minimum pension, if they were in a contracted-out scheme. Additionally, where applicable, all widows and widowers are entitled on retirement to half the graduated pension earned by their spouse.

■ Widows under 60 who remarry, or live with a man as his wife, cease to receive widows' pension. A widow who has cohabited and loses her entitlement to a widows' pension will, if the cohabitation ends, be entitled to claim it again. Widows over 60 are not affected by the rules and continue to receive their pension.

Tax and tax allowances

Widows and widowers receive the normal single person's tax allowance of £4,045 a year. If they have dependent children, they should also claim the additional personal allowance of £1,830 for single parents. Both are also entitled to any unused portion of the married couple's allowance in the year of their partner's death.

Widow's bereavement allowance. This is an extra allowance, worth £1,830 a year, specially given to widows to assist them over the first difficult period. To qualify, a widow's late husband must have been entitled to the married couple's tax allowance at the time of his death. The allowance is given both in the tax year she became widowed and in the following tax year.

N.B. Tax relief on the additional personal allowance, married couple's allowance and widow's bereavement allowance is 15 per cent.

Useful Inland Revenue leaflets. These are available from any tax office.

- IR 45: *What to Do About Tax When Someone Dies*
- IR 90: *Tax Allowances and Reliefs*
- IR 91: *A Guide for Widows and Widowers*
- IHT 3: *An Introduction to Inheritance Tax.*

Advice. Many people have difficulty in working out exactly what they are entitled to – and how to claim it. The Citizens Advice Bureau is always very helpful; as are Cruse and the National Association of Widows (see below).

Organisations that can help

Problems vary. For some, the hardest thing to bear is the loneliness of returning to an empty house. For others, money problems seem to dominate everything else. For many older women in particular, who have not got a job, widowhood creates a great gulf where for a while there is no real sense of purpose. Many widowed men and women go through a spell of feeling enraged against their partner for dying. Most are baffled and hurt by the seeming indifference of friends, who appear more embarrassed than sympathetic.

In time, all these feelings soften, problems diminish and individuals are able to recapture their joy for living with all its many pleasures. Talking to other people who know the difficulties from their own experience can be a tremendous help. The following organisations not only offer opportunities for companionship but also provide an advisory and support service.

Cruse Bereavement Care, Cruse House, 126 Sheen Road, Richmond, Surrey TW9 1UR. T:0181 940 4818. Offers free help and advice through its local branches to anyone who has been bereaved. There are also opportunities for social support plus a list of publications. For a direct link to a counsellor, telephone Cruse Bereavement Line on 0181 332 7227 (Monday – Friday, 9.30 a.m. to 5 p.m.).

National Association of Widows, 54-57 Allison Street, Digbeth, Birmingham B5 5TH. T:0121 643 8348. The Association is a national voluntary organisation which offers a free and confidential advice and information service. Membership is £5.50 a year.

Many professional and other groups offer a range of services for widows and widowers associated with them. Trade unions are often particularly supportive, as are Rotary Clubs, all the armed forces organisations and most benevolent societies. Many local Age Concern groups offer a counselling service.

Index

add after a page number indicates that the organisation's address is included in that reference. References in italics indicate tables.